CODE YOUR VIS

Mastering Zig For Real-World Applications

BENJAMIN SAMUEL

TABLE OF CONTENT

PREFACE

Hey there, future Zigonaut! If you've picked up this book, chances are you're either curious about the buzz surrounding this intriguing language, or perhaps you've already dipped your toes in and are now ready to truly understand its power. Well, you've landed in the right place. Think of this not just as a technical manual, but as your friendly guide, your patient mentor, as we embark on an exciting expedition together – a journey into the very essence of Zig.

Now, you might be thinking, "Another programming book? What makes this one different?" And that's a fair question. See, Zig isn't just another language vying for attention in the crowded landscape of software development. It's got a different philosophy, a unique soul, if you will. It's about control, about understanding what's happening under the hood, about building software that's not only blazingly fast but also remarkably reliable. It's a language that whispers promises of performance without sacrificing clarity, a language that empowers you with low-level capabilities while offering a surprisingly approachable high-level experience.

Remember that feeling? That moment you envisioned your project finally taking shape, running with incredible speed, flawlessly handling every task you throw at it? Maybe it's a lightning-fast game engine you've always dreamed of building, or a rock-solid embedded system that just *works*, or perhaps even a cutting-edge networking application that handles immense traffic with grace. Picture it vividly for a moment. Feel the satisfaction of your creation humming with efficiency, the elegance of its design, the sheer power at your fingertips.

Now, what if I told you that the language you hold in your hands – Zig – is a key that can unlock that very vision? It's the tool that can bridge the gap between your ambitious ideas and their tangible, high-performing reality. It's about having the right level of abstraction, precisely when you need it, without the hidden magic that can often lead to unexpected behavior and frustrating debugging sessions.

In the pages that follow, we won't just throw syntax and concepts at you. We'll explore the *why* behind Zig's design decisions. We'll peel back the layers, revealing the elegance and the intentionality that make this language so compelling. We'll start with the fundamentals, building a solid foundation step by step, and then gradually venture into more advanced territories, uncovering the true potential that Zig holds.

Think of it as learning to build with a set of exquisitely crafted tools. You'll understand how each tool works, its strengths, and how to wield it with precision. You won't just be writing code; you'll be architecting solutions with a deep understanding of the underlying system.

Imagine yourself confidently navigating memory management, effortlessly harnessing concurrency, and seamlessly interacting with the operating system – all with a language that feels both powerful and surprisingly intuitive. Feel that sense of mastery, that feeling of being truly in control of your craft.

The path to that feeling, to that reality, starts right here. The knowledge, the techniques, the insights – they're all within these pages, waiting to be discovered. The only thing standing between you and the exhilarating power of Zig, between your vision of a high-performance, reliable application and its actualization, is turning the page.

So, are you ready to take that first step? Are you eager to unlock the potential that lies within you and within this remarkable language?

Then get ready, because in the very next chapter, we'll begin our journey at the absolute beginning, laying the groundwork for the incredible things you'll be able to build. But be warned… what you'll discover might just change the way you think about programming forever.

CHAPTER 1

Embracing the Zig Philosophy

1.1 Why Zig? Core Principles and Design Goals

Alright, let's dive into the heart of Zig with the question: **Why Zig? Core Principles and Design Goals.**

To truly understand Zig and why someone would choose it, we need to look at the foundational ideas that shaped its creation. Zig isn't just another programming language; it was designed with specific goals in mind, often as a reaction to perceived shortcomings in other languages, particularly C and C++.

Here are the core principles and design goals that underpin Zig:

1. Simplicity and Readability:

Goal: To create a language that is easier to understand, learn, and maintain compared to languages with similar capabilities.

Explanation: Zig strives for a minimal and orthogonal design. "Orthogonal" means that different features of the language can be combined in a consistent and predictable way without unexpected interactions. This reduces complexity and makes the language more intuitive. Zig avoids hidden control flow and implicit behavior, making the code's execution path clearer. The syntax is also designed to be straightforward and less verbose than some of its contemporaries.

Example: Consider memory management. In C++, you have manual memory management with `new` and `delete`, smart pointers, and garbage collection as possibilities. This can lead to confusion about which approach is being used. Zig, on the other hand, has explicit manual memory management but provides powerful tools (like allocators) to manage it effectively and safely without hidden mechanisms. The code clearly shows where memory is being allocated and deallocated.

Code snippet

```
// Zig example: Explicit memory allocation
const std = @import("std");

pub fn main() !void {
                                    const        allocator        =
std.heap.ArenaAllocator.init(std.heap.page_allocator, 1024);
    defer allocator.deinit();
    const arena = allocator.allocator();

    const my_int = try arena.create(i32);
    my_int.* = 42;
    std.debug.print("The value is: {}\n", .{my_int.*});
}
```

In this simple example, the allocation is explicit through `arena.create()`, and the deallocation happens when the `ArenaAllocator` is deinitialized. There's no hidden garbage collection at play.

2. Safety:

Goal: To provide safety without sacrificing performance or requiring a garbage collector.

Explanation: Zig achieves safety through several mechanisms:

Optional Types: These help prevent null pointer exceptions by explicitly stating when a value might be absent.

Compile-Time Safety Checks: Zig performs rigorous checks at compile time to catch potential errors early.

No Implicit Type Conversions: Explicit conversions reduce the risk of unexpected behavior and data loss.

Memory Safety Tools: While memory is managed manually, Zig provides features like bounds checking (in debug builds) and clear ownership semantics to help avoid common memory-related bugs.

Example (Optional Types):

Code snippet

```
// Zig example: Optional type
fn findValue(array: []const i32, target: i32) ?usize {
   for (array, i) |value, index| {
      if (value == target) {
         return index;
      }
   }
}
```

```
    return null; // Explicitly return null if not found
}

pub fn main() !void {
    const numbers = [_]i32{1, 5, 10, 15};
    const index = findValue(&numbers, 10);

    if (index) |i| {
        std.debug.print("Value found at index: {}\n", .{i});
    } else {
        std.debug.print("Value not found.\n", .{});
    }
}
```

Here, `?usize` clearly indicates that the function might return either a `usize` (the index) or `null` if the value isn't found. The `if (index) |i|` syntax forces you to explicitly handle the case where the value might be absent, preventing a potential null pointer dereference.

3. Performance and Control:

Goal: To offer performance comparable to C while providing more safety and a better developer experience. To give the programmer fine-grained control over system resources.

Explanation: Zig's lack of a garbage collector is a key factor in achieving predictable and high performance. The explicit memory management allows developers to optimize memory usage for their specific needs. The language provides low-level capabilities, enabling direct interaction with hardware and memory when necessary. However, it does so in a safer way than traditional C by encouraging explicit handling of potential issues.

Example (Control over Memory Layout):

Code snippet

```
// Zig example: Controlling struct layout
const std = @import("std");

packed struct Data {
    a: u1,
    b: u7,
    c: u8,
}

pub fn main() !void {
    const data = Data{ .a = 1, .b = 10, .c = 200 };
    std.debug.print("Size of Data: {} bytes\n", .{@sizeOf(Data)});
}
```

The `packed struct` keyword tells the compiler to minimize padding between the fields, giving the programmer explicit control over the memory layout, which can be crucial for performance and interoperability with hardware or other languages.

4. Interoperability with C:

Goal: To have excellent interoperability with C code, both for leveraging existing C libraries and for using Zig in projects that already have a C codebase.

Explanation: Zig can seamlessly import C headers and call C functions, and Zig code can be easily called from C. This makes it a viable option for incrementally adopting Zig in existing projects or for utilizing the vast ecosystem of C libraries. Zig aims to be a better C in many aspects while still being able to work with the existing C world.

Example (Importing C Header - Conceptual):

Code snippet

```
// Zig example: Importing a C header (hypothetical)
extern "c" {
    fn printf(format: [*c]const u8, ...) c_int;
}

pub fn main() !void {
    _ = printf("Hello from Zig!\n", .{});
}
```

While this is a simplified example, Zig allows you to declare and use C functions directly within your Zig code, making integration straightforward.

5. Pragmatism:

Goal: To be a practical language that solves real-world problems and is enjoyable to use.

Explanation: Zig's design decisions are often driven by practical considerations. The language aims to avoid unnecessary complexity and focuses on providing the tools that developers actually need. The growing standard library and the active community contribute to making Zig a practical choice for various types of projects.

In summary, Zig strives to be a modern systems programming language that offers a sweet spot between the low-level control and performance of C and the safety and developer experience of higher-level languages, all without the complexities of a garbage collector or hidden magic. Its core principles revolve around simplicity, safety, performance, excellent C interoperability, and a pragmatic approach to language design.

1.2 Setting Up Your Zig Development Environment (Installation & Tools)

Alright, let's get our hands dirty and talk about **Setting Up Your Zig Development Environment (Installation & Tools)**. Before you can start coding your vision in Zig, you need to get the necessary tools installed on your system. The good news is that the Zig team provides relatively straightforward installation methods.

Here's a breakdown of the installation process and some essential tools you'll likely use:

1. Installation:

Zig provides pre-built binaries for various operating systems (Windows, macOS, Linux). The recommended way to install Zig is usually through downloading these official releases.

Downloading the Binary:

Go to the official Zig downloads page: https://ziglang.org/download/

Choose the appropriate pre-built binary for your operating system and architecture (e.g., `zig-linux-x86_64.tar.xz` for 64-bit Linux, `zig-macos-x86_64.tar.xz` or `zig-macos-aarch64.tar.xz` for macOS, `zig-windows-x86_64.zip` for 64-bit Windows).

Download the file.

Extracting the Binary:

Linux/macOS: Open your terminal and navigate to the directory where you downloaded the file. Use the `tar` command to extract it. For example:

Bash

```
tar xvf zig-linux-x86_64.tar.xz
# or
tar xvf zig-macos-x86_64.tar.xz
# or
tar xvf zig-macos-aarch64.tar.xz
```

This will create a directory named something like `zig-linux-x86_64` (the exact name depends on the version).

Windows: Extract the contents of the downloaded ZIP file to a directory of your choice (e.g., `C:\zig`).

Adding Zig to Your System's PATH: This step is crucial so that you can run the `zig` command from any terminal or command prompt without having to navigate to the Zig directory every time.

Linux/macOS:

Open your shell configuration file (e.g., `~/.bashrc`, `~/.zshrc`).

Add the following line, replacing `/path/to/zig` with the actual path to the extracted Zig directory:

Bash

```
export PATH="$PATH:/path/to/zig"
```

Save the file and then either close and reopen your terminal or run `source ~/.bashrc` (or `source ~/.zshrc`).

Windows:

Search for "environment variables" in the Start Menu and open "Edit the system environment variables."

Click the "Environment Variables..." button.

In the "System variables" section, find[1] the variable named "Path" and select it.

Click the "Edit..." button.

Click "New" and add the path to the Zig directory (e.g., `C:\zig`).

Click "OK" on all the dialogs. You might need to restart your command prompt or PowerShell for the changes to take effect.

Verifying the Installation:

Open a new terminal or command prompt.

Run the following command:

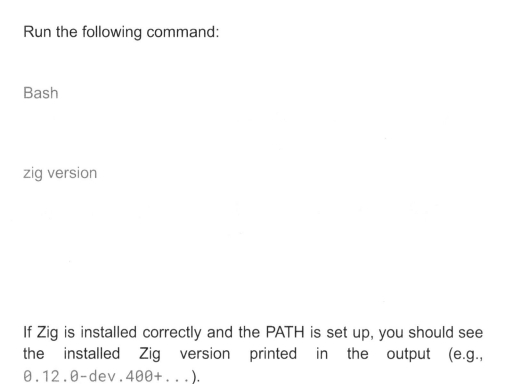

Bash

zig version

If Zig is installed correctly and the PATH is set up, you should see the installed Zig version printed in the output (e.g., `0.12.0-dev.400+...`).

2. Essential Tools:

Once you have Zig installed, you'll likely interact with it through a few core tools:

The `zig` Command-Line Interface (CLI): This is your primary tool for interacting with the Zig compiler and build system. Here are some common `zig` commands you'll use frequently:

`zig build-exe <source_file>.zig`: Compiles your Zig source file into an executable.

Bash

zig build-exe main.zig

This will create an executable file (e.g., `main` on Linux/macOS, `main.exe` on Windows).

`zig run <source_file>.zig`: Compiles and immediately runs your Zig source file. This is convenient for quick tests.

Bash

zig run hello.zig

`zig build`: Executes the build process defined in a `build.zig` file (which we'll likely cover later for more complex projects).

`zig test <source_file>.zig`: Runs the tests defined in your Zig source file.

`zig fmt <source_file>.zig`: Formats your Zig code according to the standard Zig style. This helps maintain code consistency.

`zig doc <source_file>.zig`: Generates documentation from your Zig code comments.

`zig version`: Displays the installed Zig version.

Text Editor or Integrated Development Environment (IDE): While you can write Zig code in any plain text editor, using a code editor with Zig language support will greatly enhance your development experience. Features like syntax highlighting, code completion, error checking, and debugging integration can significantly improve productivity. Some popular options include:

Visual Studio Code (VS Code): A highly popular and extensible editor with excellent Zig language support through extensions like "Zig Language Support" by Zig Tools.

Neovim: A powerful and highly configurable text editor with growing Zig support through plugins.

Vim: Similar to Neovim, with Zig syntax highlighting and other plugins available.

JetBrains IntelliJ IDEA with the Zig plugin: IntelliJ IDEA offers robust IDE features, and there's a Zig plugin available for it.

Setting up Zig language support in your chosen editor usually involves installing a specific extension or configuring syntax highlighting rules. Refer to the documentation of your editor and the Zig extension you choose for detailed instructions.

Build System (build.zig): For more complex projects with multiple source files, dependencies, and build steps, Zig uses a `build.zig` file at the root of your project. This file is written in Zig itself and defines how your project should be built, tested, and packaged. We'll delve into `build.zig` in more detail later, but it's an essential tool for managing larger Zig projects.

In summary, setting up your Zig development environment involves:

1.**Downloading** the appropriate Zig binary for your system.

2. **Extracting** the downloaded archive.

3. **Adding the Zig directory to your system's PATH** environment variable.

4. **Verifying the installation** using `zig version`.

5. Choosing and setting up a **text editor or IDE** with Zig language support.

6. Familiarizing yourself with the basic `zig` **CLI commands**.

7. Understanding that for larger projects, you'll use the `build.zig` **build system**.

With these steps completed, you'll have a working Zig development environment ready to bring your coding visions to life! Don't hesitate to ask if you encounter any issues during the installation process or if you have questions about any of these tools. Next, we can move on to the very basics of the Zig language itself.

1.3 Your First "Hello, Zig!" and Understanding the Basics

Now that you have Zig installed, let's write your very first "Hello, Zig!" program and break down some of the fundamental concepts you encounter.

1. Creating Your First Zig File:

Open your text editor or IDE.

Create a new file and save it as hello.zig.

Type the following code into the file:

Code snippet

```
const std = @import("std");

pub fn main() !void {
    std.debug.print("Hello, Zig!\n", .{});
}
```

2. Running Your "Hello, Zig!" Program:

Open your terminal or command prompt.

Navigate to the directory where you saved `hello.zig`.

Run the following command:

Bash

```
zig run hello.zig
```

You should see the output:

```
Hello, Zig!
```

Congratulations! You've just run your first Zig program. Now, let's break down what's happening in this simple piece of code:

3. Understanding the Basics:

```
const std = @import("std");:
```

`const`: This keyword declares a constant variable named `std`. In Zig, constants must be initialized at compile time and their values cannot be changed later.

`std`: This is the name we've chosen for our constant. It's a common convention to name the standard library import as `std`.

`@import("std")`: This is a built-in Zig function (identified by the @ symbol) that imports the Zig standard library. The standard library provides a wide range of functionalities, including input/output, memory management, data structures, and more. Think of it like importing modules or packages in other languages.

`pub fn main() !void { ... }`:

`pub`: This keyword makes the `main` function public, meaning it can be accessed from outside the current file (though in a simple single-file program, this isn't strictly necessary). For executable programs, the `main` function serves as the entry point of the program's execution.

`fn`: This keyword declares a function named `main`.

`()`: These parentheses indicate that the `main` function doesn't take any arguments.

`!void`: This specifies the return type of the `main` function.

`void`: Indicates that the function doesn't return a normal value.

`!`: This signifies that the function can potentially return an error. In this case, if something goes wrong during the execution of `main`, it could result in an error. For this simple "Hello, Zig!" program, errors are unlikely, but it's good practice to include the `!` as the entry point of an executable might interact with the operating system, which can lead to errors.

```
std.debug.print("Hello, Zig!\n", .{});:
```

`std`: We are accessing the standard library that we imported earlier.

`.debug`: This is a module within the standard library that provides utilities for debugging.

`.print`: This is a function within the `std.debug` module used for printing formatted output to the standard output stream (usually your terminal).

`("Hello, Zig!\n", .{})`: These are the arguments passed to the `std.debug.print` function.

"Hello, Zig!\n": This is the format string. It's similar to printf in C. The \n is an escape sequence that represents a newline character, so the output will end with a line break.

.{}: This is an empty anonymous struct literal. The std.debug.print function uses this to pass arguments that will be substituted into the format string. In this case, there are no placeholders in the format string (like {}), so an empty struct is passed. For more complex output, you would include placeholders and the corresponding values in this struct. For example: std.debug.print("The answer is: {}\n", .{ 42 });.

Key Takeaways from This Example:

Importing Libraries: You use @import to bring in external code, like the standard library.

The main Function: This is the starting point of your executable Zig programs.

Function Declaration: You use the fn keyword to define functions, specifying their name, parameters (if any), and return type.

Constants: Use const to declare variables whose values won't change.

Standard Library: The std library provides essential functionalities.

Printing Output: `std.debug.print` is a common way to display information during development.

Error Handling (Implicit): The `!` in the `main` function's return type indicates potential errors, a core aspect of Zig's design philosophy.

This simple "Hello, Zig!" program lays the groundwork for understanding more complex Zig code. As we move forward, you'll encounter these fundamental building blocks repeatedly.

CHAPTER 2

The Fundamentals of Zig Language

2.1 Variables, Data Types, and Mutability in Zig

Okay, let's try explaining **Variables, Data Types, and Mutability in Zig** from a slightly different angle, perhaps using an analogy and focusing on the core ideas in a more conceptual way.

Imagine you have containers in your programming world. These containers are where you store information. In Zig, these containers are called **variables**.

Variables: Your Information Holders

Think of a variable as a labeled box. You give it a name (the variable name), and you can put something inside it (the value).

Declaring a box: Before you can put anything in a box, you need to declare it. In Zig, you use the keyword `var` to say, "Hey, I want a box with this name."

Code snippet

```
var myNumber; // Declaring a box named 'myNumber'
var myText;   // Declaring a box named 'myText'
```

Putting something in the box (initialization): When you first create a box, you usually put something in it. This is called initialization. Zig can sometimes guess what kind of thing you're putting in the box based on the initial value.

Code snippet

```
var age = 30;     // Box named 'age' now holds the number 30
var message = "Hi"; // Box named 'message' now holds the text "Hi"
```

Data Types: Knowing What Kind of Stuff Goes in the Box

Now, imagine that some boxes are designed to hold specific kinds of things. A box labeled "Numbers Only" shouldn't have text in it. In programming, the "kind of thing" a variable can hold is called its **data type**.

Zig is pretty strict about this. Once you decide a box is for numbers, you can't just put text in it without explicitly saying you want to change the type (which isn't always straightforward or allowed).

Here are some common "box types" (data types) in Zig:

Whole Number Boxes: These are for integers (like -5, 0, 100). Zig has different sizes for these boxes (small, medium, large) and can hold positive and negative (i8, i32) or only non-negative (u8, u32) numbers. Think of it as different sized containers for whole items.

Decimal Number Boxes: These are for numbers with decimal points (like 3.14, -0.5). Zig has different precisions for these (f32, f64), like more precise measuring cups.

True/False Boxes: These can only hold one of two values: true or false. Think of a light switch – it's either on or off. This is the bool type.

Text Boxes: These hold sequences of characters (like words or sentences). In Zig, these are often represented as "slices" of bytes ([ ]const u8). Imagine a strip of paper with letters written on it.

Address Boxes (Pointers): These boxes don't hold the actual information, but rather the *location* of the information somewhere else. Think of a treasure map – it tells you where to find the treasure, not the treasure itself. These are pointer types (*T).

Grouped Boxes (Structs): Imagine a toolbox with different compartments. A struct allows you to group several variables (boxes) together under a single name. Each compartment can hold a different type of item.

Either/Or Boxes (Unions): These are special boxes that can hold one type of thing *or* another, but not both at the same time. It's like a special compartment that can be configured to hold either a tool *or* a snack, but not both simultaneously.

Limited Choice Boxes (Enums): These boxes can only hold one of a predefined set of values, like colors (Red, Green, Blue). It's like a box with labels inside, and you can only pick one label.

Maybe Boxes (Optionals): These boxes can either hold a value of a certain type *or* nothing at all (`null`). It's like a gift box that might contain a present, or it might be empty.

When you declare a variable, you can either explicitly say what type of box it is, or Zig can sometimes figure it out based on what you initially put inside.

Code snippet

var quantity: u32 = 5; // We're saying 'quantity' is a box for non-negative whole numbers, and we put 5 in it.
var greeting = "Hello"; // Zig sees we're putting text in, so it knows 'greeting' is a text box.

Mutability: Can You Change What's in the Box?

Now, let's talk about whether you can change the contents of a box after you've put something in it. This is called **mutability**.

`var` **- Changeable Boxes:** When you declare a variable using `var`, it's like a regular box where you can take out the old contents and put something new in.

Code snippet

var score = 100;
std.debug.print("Initial score: {}\n", .{score});
score = 150; // We changed what's in the 'score' box
std.debug.print("Updated score: {}\n", .{score});

`const` - **Unchangeable Boxes:** When you declare something using `const`, it's like a sealed box. Once you put something in it, you can't take it out and put something else in. The value is constant and cannot be reassigned after its initial setup.

Code snippet

```
const pi = 3.14159;
std.debug.print("The value of pi is: {}\n", .{pi});
// pi = 3.0; // This would be like trying to open a sealed box and would cause an error.

const name = "Charlie";
// name = "Chuck"; // Trying to put something new in the sealed 'name' box is not allowed.
```

Why is this important?

Knowing the type of information a variable holds helps Zig (and you) prevent errors. You wouldn't want to try adding text to a number directly! Mutability control (`var` vs. `const`) helps you write safer and more predictable code by clearly indicating which values are meant to stay the same and which can change. This makes it easier to reason about how your program works.

So, in essence:

Variables are like labeled boxes for storing information.

Data Types define what kind of information can go into a specific box.

Mutability (using `var` or `const`) determines whether you can change the contents of a box after it's been filled.

2.2 Operators, Expressions, and Control Flow (if, else, for, while)

Okay, let's try explaining **Operators, Expressions, and Control Flow (if, else, for, while)** using a different approach – think of it like giving instructions to a robot.

1. Operators: The Robot's Actions

Imagine operators as the specific actions your robot can perform.

Math Actions: + (add), – (subtract), * (multiply), / (divide), % (find the remainder). These tell the robot to do basic arithmetic.

"Robot, take the number 5 and the number 2, and perform the **add** action. Tell me the result." (`5 + 2`)

"Robot, what's the **remainder** when you divide 7 by 3?" (`7 % 3`)

Comparison Actions: `==` (is equal to?), `!=` (is not equal to?), `<` (is less than?), `>` (is greater than?), `<=` (is less than or equal to?), `>=` (is greater than or equal to?). These are like asking the robot to compare two things and say "yes" (true) or "no" (false).

"Robot, is the number of apples (let's say it's 5) **equal to** the number of oranges (also 5)?" (`5 == 5` -> "Yes, it's true!")

"Robot, is the temperature (20 degrees) **greater than** the freezing point (0 degrees)?" (20 > 0 -> "Yes, it's true!")

Logic Actions: and (both must be true), or (at least one must be true), ! (not / the opposite). These help the robot make more complex decisions based on multiple "yes" or "no" answers.

"Robot, is it raining **and** do I have an umbrella?" (Only "yes" if both are true)

"Robot, is it a weekday **or** is it my birthday?" ("Yes" if either one is true)

"Robot, is it **not** sunny?" ("Yes" if it's false that it's sunny)

Bit-Fiddling Actions (Lower Level): &, |, ^, <<, >>, ~. These are like very precise actions on the internal binary switches of the robot's memory – usually for advanced tasks.

Putting Values in Memory: = (assign). This tells the robot to store a value in a specific memory location (a variable).

"Robot, **store** the number 10 in the memory labeled 'count'." (count = 10)

"Robot, **add** 5 to the current value in 'count' and **store** the new result back in 'count'." (count += 5)

2. Expressions: Asking the Robot Questions or Giving Instructions that Result in a Value

An expression is like a question you ask the robot or a set of instructions that will give you back a specific result.

Simple questions/instructions: "Robot, what is the number 5?" (evaluates to 5), "Robot, what is the value stored in 'myVariable'?" (evaluates to the value in `myVariable`).

More complex questions/instructions: "Robot, what is 2 plus 3 multiplied by 4?" (`2 + 3 * 4` evaluates to 14). "Robot, is the value in 'temperature' greater than 25?" (`temperature > 25` evaluates to `true` or `false`).

The robot takes the operators and the values (operands) in an expression and performs the actions to give you a final value.

3. Control Flow: Telling the Robot How to Make Decisions and Repeat Tasks

Control flow statements are like giving the robot a set of rules on how to proceed based on conditions or how many times to do something.

`if` and `else` - The Robot's Decision Maker:

"`if` the light is green, then proceed straight. `else`, stop." This tells the robot to check a condition (is the light green?). If it's true, it does one thing; otherwise, it does something else.

You can have multiple checks with `else if`: "`if` the button is red, do action A. `else if` the button is blue, do action B. `else`, do action C."

Code snippet

```
const isGreen = true;
if (isGreen) {
    std.debug.print("Robot proceeds straight.\n", .{});
} else {
    std.debug.print("Robot stops.\n", .{});
}

const buttonColor = "blue";
if (buttonColor == "red") {
    std.debug.print("Robot does action A.\n", .{});
} else if (buttonColor == "blue") {
    std.debug.print("Robot does action B.\n", .{});
} else {
    std.debug.print("Robot does action C.\n", .{});
}
```

for - The Robot's Counter or List Processor:

"Robot, for each number from 1 to 5, print the number." This tells the robot to repeat an action a specific number of times or for each item in a list.

"Robot, for each item in the shopping list, pick it up."

Code snippet

```
for (0..3) |count| {
    std.debug.print("Robot is at step {}\n", .{count + 1}); // Robot
does this 3 times
}

const items = [_][]const u8{"apple", "banana", "cherry"};
for (items) |item| {
    std.debug.print("Robot picks up {}\n", .{item}); // Robot does this
for each item
}
```

`while` - The Robot's Conditional Looper:

"Robot, while the battery level is above 20%, keep working." This tells the robot to keep doing something as long as a certain condition is true. The robot checks the condition before each repetition.

Code snippet

```
var batteryLevel = 50;
while (batteryLevel > 20) {
            std.debug.print("Robot    working    (battery:    {}%).\n",
.{batteryLevel});
    batteryLevel -= 10; // Robot uses some battery
}
std.debug.print("Battery low, robot stops.\n", .{});
```

`break` **and** `continue` **- Robot's Loop Control:**

"`break`": "Robot, if you encounter an obstacle, stop the current task immediately." (Exits the loop).

"`continue`": "Robot, if you spill something, skip the current item and move to the next one." (Skips the rest of the current loop iteration).

Think of these control flow statements as the "programming" that tells your robot how to make decisions, repeat actions, and handle different situations it might encounter while following your instructions (your Zig code).

2.3 Functions: Defining, Calling, and Understanding Zig's Function Signatures

Alright, let's talk about **Functions: Defining, Calling, and Understanding Zig's Function Signatures**. Functions are fundamental building blocks in any programming language as they allow you to encapsulate a block of code that performs a specific task. This promotes code reusability, organization, and readability.

1. Defining Functions:

In Zig, you define a function using the `fn` keyword, followed by the function name, its parameters (if any), and its return type.

The basic syntax for defining a function in Zig is:

Code snippet

```
fn          functionName(parameterName:          ParameterType,
anotherParameter: AnotherType) ReturnType {
    // Function body: code to be executed
    return returnValue; // If the function has a return type
}
```

Let's break down each part:

`fn`: This keyword signifies the beginning of a function definition.

`functionName`: This is the identifier you'll use to call or refer to the function. Choose descriptive names that indicate the function's purpose.

`(parameterName: ParameterType, ...)`: These are the function's parameters. A function can have zero or more parameters. Each parameter consists of a name (used within the function body) followed by a colon : and its data type. If there are multiple parameters, they are separated by commas.

`ReturnType`: This specifies the data type of the value that the function will return. If a function doesn't return any value, you use `void` as the return type. You can also have ! before the return type (e.g., `!void` or `!i32`) to indicate that the function can return an error in addition to (or instead of) a normal value.

`{ ... }`: These curly braces enclose the function body, which contains the sequence of statements that will be executed when the function is called.

`return returnValue;`: If the function has a return type (other than `void`), the `return` statement is used to send a value back to the caller of the function. The type of `returnValue` must match the `ReturnType` specified in the function signature.

Examples of Function Definitions:

A function that takes two integers and returns their sum:

Code snippet

```
fn add(a: i32, b: i32) i32 {
    const sum = a + b;
    return sum;
}
```

A function that takes a name (string slice) and prints a greeting (no return value):

Code snippet

```
const std = @import("std");

fn greet(name: []const u8) void {
    std.debug.print("Hello, {}!\n", .{name});
}
```

A function that takes an age and returns `true` **if the age is 18 or older, potentially returning an error if the age is negative:**

Code snippet

```
fn isAdult(age: i32) !bool {
    if (age < 0) {
        return error.InvalidAge; // Returning a predefined error
    }
    return age >= 18;
}

// You'll learn about error handling in more detail later,
// but 'error.InvalidAge' is an example of an error value.
```

2. Calling Functions:

To execute the code inside a function, you need to "call" it by using its name followed by parentheses ( ). If the function has parameters, you need to provide the corresponding arguments (values) inside the parentheses. If the function returns a value, you can store that value in a variable or use it directly in an expression.

Examples of Calling Functions:

Calling the add **function:**

Code snippet

```
const result = add(5, 3); // Calling 'add' with arguments 5 and 3
std.debug.print("The sum is: {}\n", .{result}); // Output: The sum is:
8
```

Calling the `greet` function:

Code snippet

```
greet("Alice"); // Calling 'greet' with the argument "Alice"
// Output: Hello, Alice!
```

Calling the `isAdult` function (with basic error handling for now):

Code snippet

```
const age1 = 25;
const isAdult1 = isAdult(age1) catch |err| {
    std.debug.print("Error checking age {}: {}\n", .{age1, err});
    false; // Handle the error by assuming not an adult
};
std.debug.print("Is {} an adult? {}\n", .{age1, isAdult1}); // Output: Is
25 an adult? true
```

```
const age2 = -5;
const isAdult2 = isAdult(age2) catch |err| {
    std.debug.print("Error checking age {}: {}\n", .{age2, err});
    false; // Handle the error by assuming not an adult
};
std.debug.print("Is {} an adult? {}\n", .{age2, isAdult2}); // Output:
Error checking age -5: InvalidAge
                                            //        Is -5 an adult? false
```

3. Understanding Zig's Function Signatures:

The **function signature** refers to the part of the function definition that specifies its name, parameters (including their types), and return type. The signature provides all the necessary information about how to call and use the function.

Let's look at the signatures of our example functions:

```
fn add(a: i32, b: i32) i32
```

Name: add

Parameters: a (type i32), b (type i32)

Return Type: i32

```
fn greet(name: []const u8) void
```

Name: greet

Parameters: name (type [ ]const u8)

Return Type: void

```
fn isAdult(age: i32) !bool
```

Name: isAdult

Parameters: age (type i32)

Return Type: !bool (returns a bool or an error)

Key Aspects of Zig's Function Signatures:

Explicit Types: Zig requires you to explicitly specify the types of function parameters and the return type. This contributes to Zig's type safety and helps catch type-related errors at compile time.

Parameter Names: Parameter names are part of the function definition and are used within the function body to refer to the passed-in values. When calling the function, you provide arguments based on the order of the parameters in the signature. Zig does not support named arguments in the way some other languages do.

Return Type Specification: The return type clearly indicates what kind of value (if any) the function will produce. The void return type signifies that the function performs an action but doesn't return a meaningful value.

Error Handling in Signatures: The `!` in the return type is a crucial part of Zig's explicit error handling mechanism. It signals that the function might fail and return an error value. Callers of such functions need to handle these potential errors using constructs like `catch`.

Understanding function signatures is essential for knowing how to use functions correctly. When you see a function definition, the signature tells you:

What the function is called.

What kind of input (parameters and their types) it expects.

What kind of output (return type) it will produce, including the possibility of errors.

Functions are a powerful tool for organizing your Zig code and making it more modular and reusable. As you write more complex programs, you'll rely heavily on defining and calling functions to break down your logic into manageable pieces.

CHAPTER 3

Memory Management and Allocation in Zig

3.1 Defining and Using Structs for Organized Data

Alright, let's delve into a core aspect of Zig: **Understanding Zig's Explicit Memory Management**. This is a key differentiator and a source of both power and responsibility for the Zig programmer. Unlike languages with garbage collectors (like Go or Java) or those relying heavily on RAII (Resource Acquisition Is Initialization) with smart pointers (like C++), Zig puts memory management directly in your hands.[1]

Here's a breakdown of what "explicit memory management" means in the context of Zig:

1. No Implicit Garbage Collection:

What it means: Zig does not have an automatic background process that periodically identifies and reclaims memory that is no longer being used by the program.

Implications:

Performance Predictability: You have more control over when memory is allocated and deallocated, leading to more predictable performance without unexpected pauses caused by garbage collection cycles.[2]

Lower Overhead: The runtime environment of Zig programs is smaller and has less overhead because it doesn't need to include a garbage collector.

More Control: You have fine-grained control over how memory is organized and managed, which can be crucial for performance-critical applications or when interacting directly with hardware.[3]

Responsibility: You, the programmer, are responsible for explicitly allocating and deallocating memory when it's no longer needed.[4] Failure to do so will result in memory leaks.

2. Manual Allocation and Deallocation:

How it works: You explicitly request memory when you need it and explicitly release it when you're done with it.

Tools: Zig provides mechanisms for manual memory management, primarily through **allocators**.[5] An allocator is an object that provides functions for allocating and deallocating blocks of memory.

Standard Library Allocators: The Zig standard library (`std`) provides several built-in allocators for different purposes, such as:[6]

`std.heap.GeneralPurposeAllocator`: A general-purpose heap allocator.[7]

`std.heap.ArenaAllocator`: An allocator that allocates memory from a fixed-size arena.[8] All allocations within the arena are freed at once when the arena is deinitialized.[9] This can be very efficient for managing memory with a clear lifecycle.

`std.heap.FixedBufferAllocator`: An allocator that uses a fixed-size buffer provided by the user.[10]

`std.mem.Allocator`: An interface that defines the allocation and deallocation functions.

Allocation Functions: Allocators typically provide functions like:

`alloc(len: usize, ?alignment: u2 = @alignOf(u8))` `![*c]u8`: Allocates a block of `len` bytes, optionally with a specified alignment. Returns a pointer to the allocated memory. The `!` indicates that allocation can fail (e.g., due to insufficient memory).[11]

`create(comptime T, ?alignment: u2 = @alignOf(T))` `!*T`: Allocates memory for a single value of type T and returns a pointer to it.

`allocN(comptime T, count: usize, ?alignment: u2 = @alignOf([count]T))` `![*c]T`: Allocates memory for count values of type T and returns a pointer to the beginning of the allocated array.

Deallocation Functions: Corresponding to allocation, allocators provide functions for freeing memory:[12]

`free(ptr: [*c]u8, len: usize, ?alignment: u2 = @alignOf(u8))` `void`: Deallocates a block of `len` bytes starting at `ptr`. The alignment must match the alignment used during allocation.

`destroy(ptr: *T)` `void`: Deallocates the memory pointed to by `ptr`, which was allocated using `create`.

`freeN(ptr: [*c]T, count: usize, ?alignment: u2 = @alignOf([count]T))` `void`: Deallocates the memory for `count` values of type T starting at `ptr`, allocated using `allocN`.

Example of Manual Allocation and Deallocation using `ArenaAllocator`:

Code snippet

```
const std = @import("std");

pub fn main() !void {
    const allocator = std.heap.ArenaAllocator.init(std.heap.page_allocator, 1024);
    defer allocator.deinit(); // Ensure the arena is deinitialized when the function exits

    const arena = allocator.allocator();

    // Allocate space for an integer
```

```
    const my_int_ptr = try arena.create(i32);
    my_int_ptr.* = 42;
    std.debug.print("Integer value: {}\n", .{my_int_ptr.*});

    // Allocate space for an array of 5 floats
    const num_floats = 5;
    const float_array_ptr = try arena.allocN(f32, num_floats);
    for (0..num_floats) |i| {
        float_array_ptr[i] = @floatFromInt(i) * 1.5;
    }
                        std.debug.print("Float      array:      {}\n",
.{float_array_ptr[0..num_floats]});

        // With ArenaAllocator, we don't need to free individual
    allocations.
    // 'allocator.deinit()' at the end will free all memory allocated from
    this arena.
    }
```

3. The Role of Allocators:

Abstraction: Allocators provide an abstraction over the underlying memory management mechanisms (e.g., system calls to the operating system). You interact with the allocator's methods instead of directly making low-level memory management calls.[13]

Customization: Zig's allocator interface allows you to create custom allocators with specific allocation strategies tailored to your application's needs (e.g., for specific performance characteristics or memory usage patterns).[14]

Safety through Scoping (with `defer`**):** The `defer` keyword in Zig is often used with allocator deinitialization.[15] `defer` `allocator.deinit()` ensures that the `deinit()` function of the allocator is called when the current scope (e.g., a function) is exited, regardless of how it's exited (normal return or panic). This helps prevent memory leaks by ensuring resources are cleaned up.

4. Error Handling for Allocation:

! **Return Type:** Allocation functions in Zig often have a return type that includes !, indicating that the allocation can fail (e.g., if there isn't enough memory).[16] You need to handle these potential errors using `try` or `catch`.

5. Benefits of Explicit Memory Management in Zig:

Performance: No garbage collection pauses and fine-grained control over memory layout can lead to higher and more predictable performance.

Resource Efficiency: You only allocate the memory you need and deallocate it when you're finished, potentially leading to more efficient memory usage.[17]

Low-Level Control: Essential for systems programming, embedded development, and interacting directly with hardware.[18]

Transparency: The memory management is explicit in your code, making it clearer where allocations and deallocations happen, which can aid in debugging and understanding resource usage.[19]

6. Challenges and Responsibilities:

Memory Leaks: If you forget to deallocate memory, your program will leak memory over time, potentially leading to crashes or performance degradation.

Dangling Pointers: If you deallocate memory but still have pointers referencing that memory, using those pointers will lead to undefined behavior (crashes, incorrect data).

Complexity: Managing memory manually can add complexity to your code compared to languages with automatic memory management.[20]

In summary, Zig's explicit memory management puts you in control of when and how memory is allocated and deallocated. This is achieved primarily through the use of allocators provided by the standard library or custom-defined. While this offers significant advantages in terms of performance and control, it also comes with the responsibility of ensuring that memory is managed correctly to avoid leaks and other memory-related issues. The `defer` keyword and Zig's error handling mechanisms are crucial tools for managing this responsibility effectively.[21]

Understanding this fundamental aspect of Zig is crucial as you move forward. You'll be working with allocators frequently when dealing with dynamic data structures or any data that needs to live beyond the scope it was initially created in.

3.2 Allocators: Stack, Heap, and Custom Allocation Strategies

Now that we've established the concept of explicit memory management, let's dive deeper into **Allocators: Stack, Heap, and Custom Allocation Strategies** in Zig. Understanding these different approaches to memory allocation is key to writing efficient and reliable Zig code.

1. The Stack:

Concept: The stack is a region of memory that is managed in a Last-In, First-Out (LIFO) manner.[1] Think of it like a stack of plates – the last plate you put on top is the first one you take off.

Allocation and Deallocation: Memory on the stack is typically allocated automatically when a function is called.[2] Local variables declared within a function are usually allocated on the stack.[3] This allocation happens by simply moving the "stack pointer." When the function returns, the stack pointer is moved back, effectively deallocating all the memory used by that function's local variables. This process is very fast and efficient.

Lifespan: Memory allocated on the stack has a limited lifespan – it exists only for the duration of the function call.[4] Once the function returns, the memory is no longer considered valid.

Size: The size of the stack is usually fixed and relatively small compared to the heap.[5]

Zig and the Stack: In Zig, local variables within a function generally reside on the stack by default.[6] The compiler manages this allocation and deallocation automatically based on the function's scope. You don't explicitly allocate or deallocate stack memory using allocator APIs.

Code snippet

```
const std = @import("std");

fn exampleStack() void {
    var x: i32 = 10; // 'x' is likely allocated on the stack
```

```
    var message: [20]u8 = "Hello from stack"; // 'message' array is
also on the stack
    std.debug.print("Value of x: {}\n", .{x});
    std.debug.print("Message: {}\n", .{message});
}

pub fn main() !void {
    exampleStack();
} // When exampleStack returns, memory for x and message is
automatically 'deallocated'
```

2. The Heap:

Concept: The heap is a larger, more flexible region of memory where memory can be allocated and deallocated at any time and in any order.[7] It's like a big storage room where you can request space for items of various sizes and return that space when you're done.

Allocation and Deallocation: Memory on the heap is managed explicitly by the programmer using allocators.[8] You request a block of memory of a certain size, and the allocator finds a suitable free block on the heap and returns a pointer to it. When you're finished with the memory, you must explicitly tell the allocator to free it.

Lifespan: Memory allocated on the heap can persist beyond the scope of the function that allocated it, as long as there are still pointers referencing it.[9] It's your responsibility to manage its lifetime.

Size: The heap is typically much larger than the stack and can grow or shrink as the program runs (within system limits).[10]

Zig and the Heap: In Zig, if you need memory that outlives the current function or whose size isn't known at compile time, you'll typically allocate it from the heap using an allocator (like `std.heap.GeneralPurposeAllocator` or `std.heap.ArenaAllocator`).[11]

Code snippet

```
const std = @import("std");

pub fn main() !void {
    const allocator = std.heap.GeneralPurposeAllocator.init(std.heap.page_allocator){}.allocator();
    defer std.heap.GeneralPurposeAllocator.deinit(allocator);

    // Allocate space for 5 integers on the heap
    const num_ints = 5;
    const heap_array_ptr = try allocator.allocN(i32, num_ints);
    defer allocator.freeN(heap_array_ptr, num_ints); // Ensure it's freed

    for (0..num_ints) |i| {
        heap_array_ptr[i] = i * 2;
    }
    std.debug.print("Heap array: {}\n", .{heap_array_ptr[0..num_ints]});

    // Allocate space for a string on the heap
    const message = try allocator.alloc(u8, 10);
```

```
    defer allocator.free(message, 10);
    std.mem.copy(u8, message, "Heap string");
    std.debug.print("Heap string: {}\n", .{message});
}
```

3. Custom Allocation Strategies:

Zig's design allows for the creation of custom allocators, enabling you to implement specific memory management strategies tailored to your application's needs. This can be useful in various scenarios:

Memory Pools: Pre-allocate a large chunk of memory and then serve smaller allocations from this pool.[12] This can be faster and more predictable than general-purpose allocation for objects of a known size.

Region-Based Allocation: Allocate memory within a specific region and then free the entire region at once.[13] `ArenaAllocator` is an example of this. This can simplify memory management for objects with related lifecycles.

Specialized Allocators for Specific Data Structures: You might create an allocator optimized for a particular data structure (e.g., a linked list or a tree) to improve performance or reduce fragmentation.

Interfacing with External Memory Management: In some cases, you might need to integrate with external memory management systems or hardware-specific memory regions. Custom allocators can facilitate this.

How to Create a Custom Allocator (Conceptual):

To create a custom allocator in Zig, you would typically:

1.Define a struct that holds the state of your allocator.

2. Implement the `std.mem.Allocator` **interface for** your struct. This involves providing implementations for the `alloc`, `free`, and potentially other methods like `resize`.

Code snippet

```
const std = @import("std");

// Example of a very simple custom allocator (not fully functional)
pub const SimpleAllocator = struct {
    memory: []u8,
    used: usize,
};

pub fn simpleAllocatorInit(buffer: []u8) SimpleAllocator {
    return .{ .memory = buffer, .used = 0 };
}

pub fn simpleAllocatorAlloc(self: *SimpleAllocator, len: usize, _: u2) ![*c]u8 {
    if (self.used + len > self.memory.len) {
        return error.OutOfMemory;
    }
    const ptr = &self.memory[self.used];
    self.used += len;
    return @ptrCast([*c]u8, ptr);
}
```

```
pub fn simpleAllocatorFree(_: *SimpleAllocator, _: [*c]u8, _: usize,
_: u2) void {
    // Simple allocator doesn't track individual allocations for free
    // In a real implementation, you'd need more bookkeeping.
}

pub fn main() !void {
    var buffer: [1024]u8 = undefined;
    var allocator = simpleAllocatorInit(&buffer);

    const ptr1 = try allocator.alloc(100, 1);
    std.mem.set(u8, ptr1[0..100], 0);
    std.debug.print("Allocated 100 bytes at: {}\n", .{ptr1});

    const ptr2 = try allocator.alloc(50, 1);
    std.mem.set(u8, ptr2[0..50], 0xff);
    std.debug.print("Allocated 50 bytes at: {}\n", .{ptr2});

    // In this simple example, we don't individually free. The whole
buffer's
    // 'allocation' ends when 'allocator' goes out of scope.
}
```

Key Takeaways:

Stack: Automatic, fast, LIFO, limited lifespan (function scope).[14] Used for local variables by default.

Heap: Manual, requires allocators, flexible lifespan, larger size.[15] Used for dynamic memory and data that needs to persist.

Custom Allocators: Allow for tailored memory management strategies to optimize for specific use cases or integrate with external systems.[16]

Understanding when to use stack vs. heap and how to leverage allocators (including the possibility of creating custom ones) is crucial for writing efficient and robust Zig programs, especially in performance-sensitive or low-level contexts.

3.3 Error Handling and Resource Management in Memory Operations

Let's tackle the critical aspects of **Error Handling and Resource Management in Memory Operations** within Zig. Since Zig emphasizes explicit memory management, it's paramount to handle potential errors during allocation and to ensure that allocated resources (especially memory) are properly released to prevent leaks and other issues.[1]

1. Error Handling in Memory Allocation:

! **Return Type:** As we touched on earlier, Zig's allocation functions (like `alloc`, `allocN`, `create`) in the standard library often have a return type that includes the ! symbol. This signifies that these functions can potentially fail and return an error value instead of a valid pointer. The error could be due to various reasons, such as insufficient memory.

Handling Allocation Errors with `try` **and** `catch`: To handle these potential errors, you typically use the `try` keyword before calling an allocation function.[2] If the function returns an error, the execution jumps to a `catch` block where you can handle the error appropriately.

Code snippet

const std = @import("std");

```
pub fn main() !void {
    const allocator = std.heap.GeneralPurposeAllocator.init(std.heap.page_allocator){}.allocator();
    defer std.heap.GeneralPurposeAllocator.deinit(allocator);

    // Attempt to allocate 1MB of memory
    const large_allocation = try allocator.alloc(u8, 1024 * 1024);
    defer allocator.free(large_allocation, 1024 * 1024);
    std.debug.print("Successfully allocated 1MB.\n", .{});

    // What if allocation fails? Let's simulate a potential failure
    const too_large_allocation = allocator.alloc(u8, std.math.maxInt(usize));
    if (too_large_allocation == null) {
        std.debug.print("Failed to allocate very large amount of memory.\n", .{});
    } else {
        defer allocator.free(too_large_allocation.?, std.math.maxInt(usize));
        std.debug.print("Unexpectedly allocated a huge amount of memory!\n", .{});
    }

    // More idiomatic error handling with 'try'
    const another_large_allocation = try allocator.alloc(u8, std.math.maxInt(usize));
    defer allocator.free(another_large_allocation, std.math.maxInt(usize));
    std.debug.print("This line will likely not be reached due to out of memory.\n", .{});
}
```

In the last example, if `allocator.alloc` fails, it will return an error, and the `try` keyword will propagate this error up the call stack (in this case, causing `main` to return an error). The `!void` return type of `main` allows for this error propagation.

You can also use a `catch` block to specifically handle allocation errors:[3]

Code snippet

```
const std = @import("std");

pub fn main() !void {
    const allocator = std.heap.GeneralPurposeAllocator.init(std.heap.page_allocator){}.allocator();
    defer std.heap.GeneralPurposeAllocator.deinit(allocator);

    const very_large_allocation = allocator.alloc(u8, std.math.maxInt(usize)) catch |err| {
        std.debug.print("Allocation failed with error: {}\n", .{err});
        return; // Exit the function if allocation fails
    };
    defer allocator.free(very_large_allocation, std.math.maxInt(usize));
    std.debug.print("Successfully allocated a huge amount (if you see this, something is wrong!).\n", .{});
}
```

Checking for `null` **(Less Idiomatic for** ! **Functions):** While some allocation functions might return `null` on failure (especially in early Zig versions or for lower-level APIs), the more idiomatic approach with standard library allocators is to use the ! return type and handle errors with `try` and `catch`.

2. Resource Management (Ensuring Deallocation):

Since memory in Zig is managed manually, it's crucial to ensure that every allocation is eventually paired with a corresponding deallocation. Failing to do so leads to **memory leaks**, where your program consumes more and more memory without releasing it, potentially leading to crashes or system instability.

The `defer` **Keyword:** Zig's `defer` keyword is an invaluable tool for resource management.[4] When you use `defer` followed by a function call, that function call will be executed when the current scope (usually a function) is exited, regardless of how the scope is exited (normal return, early return, or panic).[5] This is perfect for ensuring that cleanup actions, like freeing allocated memory, are always performed.

Code snippet

```
const std = @import("std");

fn processData() !void {
    const allocator = std.heap.GeneralPurposeAllocator.init(std.heap.page_allocator){}.allocator();
    defer std.heap.GeneralPurposeAllocator.deinit(allocator);

    // Allocate some memory
```

```
    const data = try allocator.alloc(u8, 100);
        defer allocator.free(data, 100); // 'free' will be called when
processData exits

    // Use the allocated memory...
    std.mem.set(u8, data, 0);
    std.debug.print("Data processed.\n", .{});

        // If an error occurs before this point and the function returns
early,
    // 'defer allocator.free(data, 100)' will still be executed.
}

pub fn main() !void {
    try processData();
    std.debug.print("Program finished.\n", .{});
}
```

RAII (Resource Acquisition Is Initialization) Pattern (Manual Implementation): While Zig doesn't have built-in smart pointers like C++, you can manually implement the RAII pattern by creating structs that acquire resources (like memory) during their initialization and release them in a `defer` block associated with the struct's scope.

Code snippet

```
const std = @import("std");

const MemoryBuffer = struct {
```

```zig
    ptr: [*c]u8,
    len: usize,
    allocator: std.mem.Allocator,

        pub fn init(allocator: std.mem.Allocator, len: usize)
!MemoryBuffer {
        const ptr = try allocator.alloc(u8, len);
        return .{ .ptr = ptr, .len = len, .allocator = allocator };
    },

    pub fn deinit(self: *MemoryBuffer) void {
        self.allocator.free(self.ptr, self.len);
    },
};

pub fn main() !void {
                                    const          allocator          =
std.heap.GeneralPurposeAllocator.init(std.heap.page_allocator){}.
allocator();
    defer std.heap.GeneralPurposeAllocator.deinit(allocator);

    {
        var buffer = try MemoryBuffer.init(allocator, 200);
            defer buffer.deinit(); // When the inner block exits,
buffer.deinit() is called

        std.mem.set(u8, buffer.ptr, 0xff);
        std.debug.print("Buffer created and used.\n", .{});
    } // buffer.deinit() is called here, freeing the memory
    std.debug.print("Buffer memory should now be freed.\n", .{});
}
```

Arena Allocators for Grouped Lifecycles: When you have multiple allocations that have the same overall lifespan, using an `ArenaAllocator` can simplify resource management. You allocate memory from the arena as needed, and then you only need to deinitialize the entire arena when all those allocations are no longer required. This avoids the need to track and free individual allocations.

Code snippet

```
const std = @import("std");

pub fn processMultipleThings() !void {
    const arena = std.heap.ArenaAllocator.init(std.heap.page_allocator, 2048);
    defer arena.deinit();
    const arena_allocator = arena.allocator();

    const name = try arena_allocator.alloc(u8, 5);
    std.mem.copy(u8, name, "Alice");
    defer arena_allocator.free(name, 5); // Not strictly needed with ArenaAllocator

    const ages = try arena_allocator.allocN(i32, 3);
    ages[0] = 25;
    ages[1] = 30;
    ages[2] = 22;
    defer arena_allocator.freeN(ages, 3); // Not strictly needed

    std.debug.print("Processed name: {} and ages: {}\n", .{name, ages});
    // When processMultipleThings exits, arena.deinit() will free all allocations.
}
```

```
pub fn main() !void {
    try processMultipleThings();
}
```

3. Best Practices for Memory Operations:

Always Handle Allocation Errors: Use `try` and `catch` (or check for `null` if applicable) to gracefully handle situations where memory allocation fails.

Pair Allocations with Deallocations: For every `alloc`, `allocN`, or `create`, ensure there is a corresponding `free`, `freeN`, or `destroy` call.

Use `defer` for Cleanup: Employ the `defer` keyword to guarantee that deallocation functions are called when the scope is exited.[6]

Consider Arena Allocators: For groups of allocations with the same lifecycle, arena allocators can simplify management.

Be Mindful of Ownership and Lifetimes: Understand which part of your code is responsible for allocating and deallocating memory. Avoid situations where memory is freed while it's still being used (dangling pointers).

Test Thoroughly: Memory-related bugs can be subtle. Test your code carefully, especially in scenarios involving dynamic memory.

Proper error handling and diligent resource management are crucial for writing robust and reliable Zig programs that interact with memory. By understanding the potential for allocation failures and by consistently ensuring that allocated memory is freed, you can avoid common pitfalls and build stable applications.

CHAPTER 4

Structs, Unions, and Enums: Building Data Structures

4.1 Defining and Using Structs for Organized Data

Alright, let's dive into **Defining and Using Structs for Organized Data** in Zig. Structs are a fundamental way to create custom data types that group together related pieces of information under a single name. They help in organizing complex data and making your code more readable and maintainable.

1. Defining Structs:

In Zig, you define a struct using the `struct` keyword followed by the struct name and a block `{}` containing the definitions of its fields (members). Each field has a name and a specific data type.

The basic syntax for defining a struct is:

Code snippet

```
const StructName = struct {
    fieldName1: FieldType1,
    fieldName2: FieldType2,
    // ... more fields
};
```

`const StructName = struct { ... };`: This declares a constant named `StructName` that holds the definition of the struct type. It's a common convention to use PascalCase (e.g., `Person`, `Point`) for struct names.

`fieldName1: FieldType1, ...:` Inside the curly braces, you define the fields of the struct. Each field has a name (`fieldName1`) and a data type (`FieldType1`), separated by a colon. Fields are separated by commas.

Examples of Struct Definitions:

A struct to represent a point in 2D space:

Code snippet

```
const Point = struct {
    x: i32,
    y: i32,
};
```

A struct to represent a person with a name and age:

Code snippet

```
const Person = struct {
    name: []const u8,
    age: u32,
```

```
};
```

A struct with different data types:

```
const Product = struct {
    id: u64,
    name: [64]u8,
    price: f32,
    in_stock: bool,
};
```

2. Creating Instances of Structs:

Once you've defined a struct type, you can create instances (variables) of that type. There are a couple of ways to do this:

Using a struct literal: This involves providing values for each field within curly braces, prefixed with a dot and the field name.

```
var p1 = Point{ .x = 10, .y = 20 };
var alice = Person{ .name = "Alice", .age = 30 };
```

```
var laptop = Product{ .id = 12345, .name = "Awesome Laptop",
.price = 1200.50, .in_stock = true };
```

The order of field initialization in a struct literal doesn't matter as long as you use the . followed by the field name. You must initialize all fields unless they have default values (which we'll discuss later).

Declaring a variable of the struct type and then assigning values to its fields:

Code snippet

```
var p2: Point = undefined; // Declare a variable of type Point
without initial values
p2.x = 5;
p2.y = -5;

var bob: Person = undefined;
bob.name = "Bob";
bob.age = 25;
```

Note the use of undefined to declare a variable without an initial value. You must assign values to all fields before using the struct instance.

3. Accessing Struct Fields:

You can access the individual fields of a struct instance using the dot (.) operator followed by the field name.

Code snippet

```
const std = @import("std");

pub fn main() !void {
    const point = Point{ .x = 15, .y = 8 };
        std.debug.print("Point x: {}, y: {}\n", .{point.x, point.y}); //
Accessing point.x and point.y

    var person = Person{ .name = "Charlie", .age = 35 };
        std.debug.print("Person name: {}, age: {}\n", .{person.name,
person.age});
    person.age += 1; // Modifying a mutable struct field
    std.debug.print("Updated age: {}\n", .{person.age});
}
```

4. Struct Mutability:

The mutability of a struct instance is determined by whether the variable holding the instance is declared with var (mutable) or const (immutable). If the struct variable is const, you cannot change the values of its fields after initialization.

Code snippet

```
const immutable_point = Point{ .x = 1, .y = 2 };
// immutable_point.x = 5; // This would result in a compile-time
error

var mutable_point = Point{ .x = -1, .y = -2 };
mutable_point.x = 5; // This is allowed
```

5. Nested Structs:

You can define structs that contain other structs as fields, allowing you to model more complex relationships between data.

Code snippet

```
const Color = struct {
    r: u8,
    g: u8,
    b: u8,
};

const Circle = struct {
    center: Point, // Using the Point struct as a field
    radius: f32,
    fill_color: Color,
};

pub fn main() !void {
    const my_circle = Circle{
        .center = Point{ .x = 0, .y = 0 },
        .radius = 5.0,
        .fill_color = Color{ .r = 255, .g = 0, .b = 0 },
    };

    std.debug.print("Circle center x: {}, y: {}\n", .{my_circle.center.x, my_circle.center.y});
    std.debug.print("Circle radius: {}\n", .{my_circle.radius});
    std.debug.print("Fill color (R, G, B): ({}, {}, {})\n", .{my_circle.fill_color.r, my_circle.fill_color.g, my_circle.fill_color.b});
}
```

6. Anonymous Structs:

Zig allows you to define structs without giving them a name. These are often used for one-off data groupings, especially in function calls or returns.

Code snippet

```
const std = @import("std");

fn printCoordinates(coords: struct { x: f32, y: f32 }) void {
        std.debug.print("Coordinates (x: {}, y: {})\n", .{coords.x, coords.y});
}

pub fn main() !void {
    const origin = .{ .x = 0.0, .y = 0.0 }; // Anonymous struct literal
    printCoordinates(origin);

        printCoordinates(.{ .x = 1.5, .y = -2.3 }); // Passing an anonymous struct directly
}
```

7. Default Field Values (as of newer Zig versions):

In more recent versions of Zig, you can specify default values for struct fields during the definition. If you don't provide a value for such a field when creating an instance, it will be initialized with its default.

Code snippet

```
const Configuration = struct {
    timeout_ms: u32 = 5000, // Default value of 5000
    max_retries: u8 = 3,    // Default value of 3
    verbose: bool = false,  // Default value of false
};
```

```
pub fn main() !void {
    const default_config = Configuration{}; // Uses all default values
    std.debug.print("Default timeout: {}, retries: {}, verbose: {}\n",
.{default_config.timeout_ms,        default_config.max_retries,
default_config.verbose});

    const custom_config = Configuration{ .timeout_ms = 1000 }; //
Overrides timeout, uses defaults for others
    std.debug.print("Custom timeout: {}, retries: {}, verbose: {}\n",
.{custom_config.timeout_ms,        custom_config.max_retries,
custom_config.verbose});
}
```

Benefits of Using Structs:

Organization: Group related data together, making your code more structured and easier to understand.

Readability: Using meaningful field names improves the clarity of your code.

Maintainability: Changes to related data can be localized within the struct definition.

Type Safety: Structs define a specific type, allowing the compiler to catch type errors.

Abstraction: You can treat a struct as a single entity, abstracting away the individual fields.

Structs are a fundamental tool for creating your own data types in Zig and are essential for building more complex and organized programs. You'll use them extensively to represent entities, configurations, and various forms of structured data.

4.2 Exploring Unions for Type Flexibility and Memory Layout

Alright, let's delve into **Exploring Unions for Type Flexibility and Memory Layout** in Zig. Unions are another way to define custom data types, but they differ significantly from structs in how they use memory. Understanding unions is crucial for situations where a variable might hold one of several different types of data, and you need to be mindful of memory layout.

1. Defining Unions:

In Zig, you define a union using the `union` keyword followed by the union name and a block `{}` containing the definitions of its fields (members). Like structs, each field has a name and a specific data type.

The basic syntax for defining a union is:

Code snippet

```
const UnionName = union {
    field1: FieldType1,
    field2: FieldType2,
    // ... more fields
};
```

`const UnionName = union { ... };`: This declares a constant named `UnionName` that holds the definition of the union type. Conventionally, union names also follow PascalCase.

`field1 : FieldType1, . . .`: Inside the curly braces, you define the possible fields of the union. Each field has a name and a data type.

Key Difference from Structs: Memory Sharing

The crucial difference between a struct and a union is how they allocate memory for their fields.

Struct: Each field in a struct gets its own separate memory location. The size of a struct is typically the sum of the sizes of its fields (plus any padding for alignment).

Union: All fields in a union share the *same* memory location. The size of a union is determined by the size of its *largest* field. Only one field of a union is considered "active" or valid at any given time.

Examples of Union Definitions:

A union that can hold either an integer or a float:

Code snippet

```
const IntOrFloat = union {
    integer: i32,
    float: f32,
};
```

A union that can represent different types of data packets:

Code snippet

```
const DataPacket = union {
    control: struct { command: u8, flags: u8 },
    sensor_reading: struct { sensor_id: u16, value: f64 },
    text_message: [64]u8,
};
```

2. Creating Instances of Unions:

You create instances of unions using a similar syntax to structs, but you only initialize the field that you want to be active.

Code snippet

```
var value1 = IntOrFloat{ .integer = 42 }; // 'value1' now holds an integer
var value2 = IntOrFloat{ .float = 3.14 };   // 'value2' now holds a float

var packet1 = DataPacket{ .control = .{ .command = 0x01, .flags = 0x00 } }; // 'packet1' is a control packet
var packet2 = DataPacket{ .sensor_reading = .{ .sensor_id = 100, .value = 27.5 } }; // 'packet2' is a sensor reading
var packet3 = DataPacket{ .text_message = "Hello, data!" }; // 'packet3' is a text message
```

3. Accessing Union Fields:

You access the fields of a union instance using the dot (.) operator, just like with structs. However, it's crucial to know which field is currently active. Accessing an inactive field will lead to undefined behavior (you'll likely get garbage data or a crash).

Code snippet

```
const std = @import("std");

pub fn main() !void {
    var data = IntOrFloat{ .integer = 100 };
    std.debug.print("Integer value: {}\n", .{data.integer});

    data.float = 2.71828; // Now the 'float' field is active, the 'integer'
field is no longer valid
    std.debug.print("Float value: {}\n", .{data.float});
    //  std.debug.print("Integer value (after float set): {}\n",
.{data.integer}); // This would likely print garbage

    var packet = DataPacket{ .control = .{ .command = 0x05, .flags
= 0x01 } };
    std.debug.print("Control command: {}, flags: {}\n",
.{packet.control.command, packet.control.flags});

    packet.sensor_reading.sensor_id = 200;
    packet.sensor_reading.value = 98.6; // Now it's a sensor reading
    std.debug.print("Sensor ID: {}, Value: {}\n",
.{packet.sensor_reading.sensor_id,
packet.sensor_reading.value});
}
```

4. Tracking the Active Union Field (Tagged Unions):

Because only one field of a union is valid at a time, it's often necessary to keep track of which field is currently active. A common way to do this is by using an **enum** as a "tag" within a struct that contains the union. This pattern is known as a **tagged union** or **discriminated union**.

Code snippet

```
const std = @import("std");

const Value = struct {
    type: enum { Int, Float, Text },
    data: union {
        integer: i32,
        float: f32,
        text: [32]u8,
    },
};

pub fn printValue(value: Value) void {
    switch (value.type) {
        .Int => std.debug.print("Integer: {}\n", .{value.data.integer}),
        .Float => std.debug.print("Float: {}\n", .{value.data.float}),
        .Text => std.debug.print("Text: {}\n", .{value.data.text}),
    }
}

pub fn main() !void {
    var int_value = Value{ .type = .Int, .data = .{ .integer = -10 } };
    var float_value = Value{ .type = .Float, .data = .{ .float = 1.618 } };
    var text_value = Value{ .type = .Text, .data = .{ .text = "Hello Union!" } };

    printValue(int_value);
    printValue(float_value);
    printValue(text_value);
```

```
    int_value.type = .Float; // Changing the active type
    int_value.data.float = 2.0;
    printValue(int_value); // Now prints a float
}
```

In this example, the `Value` struct has a `type` field (an enum indicating the active type) and a `data` field (the union holding the actual value). The `printValue` function uses a `switch` statement on the `type` to determine which field of the union to access safely.

5. Memory Layout Considerations:

Unions are particularly useful when you need to interpret the same block of memory in different ways or when you want to save memory by having different data types share the same space.

Size of a Union: The size of a union is equal to the size of its largest field. The compiler will allocate enough space to hold any of the union's members.

Alignment: The alignment of a union is typically the strictest alignment requirement of any of its fields.

Example of Memory Layout (Conceptual):

Consider the `IntOrFloat` union (assuming i32 and f32 have the same size, say 4 bytes). An instance of `IntOrFloat` will occupy 4 bytes in memory. If you set the `integer` field, those 4 bytes will be interpreted as an integer. If you then set the `float` field, the same 4 bytes will now be interpreted as a floating-point number. The bit pattern in those 4 bytes will change based on the value you assign.

Use Cases for Unions:

Interfacing with C: Unions in Zig often directly correspond to unions in C, making interoperability easier when dealing with C APIs that use unions.

Low-Level Programming: When working with hardware or binary data formats, you might use unions to interpret the same sequence of bytes as different types of fields.

Saving Memory: If you have a situation where a variable will only ever hold one of several possible types, using a union (especially within a tagged union) can be more memory-efficient than allocating space for the largest possible struct that could hold all the alternatives.

Type Flexibility: When you need a variable that can hold different types of data at different times during the program's execution (though you need to carefully manage which type is currently active).

Important Considerations:

Undefined Behavior: Accessing the inactive field of a union is undefined behavior and can lead to unpredictable results.

Manual Tracking: You are responsible for tracking which field of a union is currently active, often by using a tagged union pattern.

Careful Use: Unions should be used with caution and a clear understanding of the memory implications. Misusing them can lead to subtle and hard-to-debug errors.

Unions in Zig provide a powerful way to work with memory flexibly and to represent data that can take on different forms. However, this flexibility comes with the responsibility of carefully managing the active type, often through the use of tagged unions, to ensure the correctness and safety of your code.

4.3 Leveraging Enums and Optionals for State Management and Safety

Alright, let's explore how **Leveraging Enums and Optionals for State Management and Safety** in Zig can lead to more robust and understandable code. These two features are powerful tools for representing different states within your program and for handling the possibility of a value being absent.

1. Enums (Enumerations) for State Management:

Enums in Zig allow you to define a type that can take on one of a finite set of named values. This is incredibly useful for representing different states or categories within your application, making your code more readable and less prone to errors compared to using raw integer constants or strings.

Defining Enums:

You define an enum using the enum keyword followed by the enum name and a block {} containing the names of the possible values (variants).

Code snippet

```
const State = enum {
    Idle,
    Loading,
    Ready,
    Error,
};

const TrafficLight = enum {
    Red,
```

```
    Yellow,
    Green,
};

const Result = enum(err: Error) { // Enums can have associated
error types
    Ok,
    Err,
};

const Error = enum {
    FileNotFound,
    NetworkError,
    InvalidData,
};
```

Basic Enums: The first two examples (`State` and `TrafficLight`) define simple enums where each variant is just a named constant.

Enums with Associated Error Types: The `Result` enum demonstrates a more advanced feature where an enum can be parameterized with an error type. This allows you to associate specific error information with an `Err` variant (though we'll see a more idiomatic way to handle results with `!void` and `error` sets later).

Using Enums:

You can declare variables of an enum type and assign them one of the defined variants using the enum name followed by a dot and the variant name.

Code snippet

```
var current_state: State = .Idle;
var light_color: TrafficLight = .Yellow;
var operation_result: Result = .Ok;

std.debug.print("Current state: {}\n", .{current_state});
std.debug.print("Light color: {}\n", .{light_color});
std.debug.print("Operation result: {}\n", .{operation_result});
```

Switching on Enums for State Management:

The `switch` statement is particularly powerful when used with enums. It allows you to execute different code blocks based on the current value of an enum variable, ensuring that you handle all possible states.

Code snippet

```
const std = @import("std");

fn handleState(state: State) void {
    switch (state) {
        .Idle => std.debug.print("System is idle.\n", .{}),
        .Loading => std.debug.print("Loading data...\n", .{}),
        .Ready => std.debug.print("System is ready.\n", .{}),
        .Error => std.debug.print("An error occurred!\n", .{}),
    }
}

fn getNextTrafficLight(current: TrafficLight) TrafficLight {
    return switch (current) {
        .Red => .Green,
        .Yellow => .Red,
        .Green => .Yellow,
    };
}
```

```zig
pub fn main() !void {
    var app_state: State = .Loading;
    handleState(app_state);
    app_state = .Ready;
    handleState(app_state);
    app_state = .Error;
    handleState(app_state);

    var light = TrafficLight.Red;
    std.debug.print("Current light: {}\n", .{light});
    light = getNextTrafficLight(light);
    std.debug.print("Next light: {}\n", .{light});
}
```

Safety Benefits of Enums:

Type Safety: The compiler ensures that you only assign valid variants of the enum to a variable of that enum type. This prevents errors that could occur if you were using raw integers or strings to represent states.

Readability: Using named variants (e.g., `.Loading` instead of 0) makes your code much more self-documenting and easier to understand.

Exhaustive Switching: The `switch` statement in Zig can enforce exhaustiveness when used with enums (with the `else` or `=>` `unreachable` clause), helping you ensure that you handle all possible states, reducing the risk of unhandled cases.

2. Optionals for Representing Absent Values:

Optionals in Zig provide a type-safe way to represent a value that might be present or absent (`null`). This helps prevent the infamous "null pointer exception" that plagues many other languages.

Defining Optional Types:

You create an optional type by prefixing a type with a question mark ?. ?T is syntactic sugar for `?T = union(null) { null, some: T };`.

Code snippet

var maybe_number: ?i32 = null; // 'maybe_number' can hold an i32 or null
var optional_name: ?[]const u8 = "John"; // 'optional_name' can hold a string or null
var optional_point: ?Point = null; // Assuming 'Point' is a struct we defined earlier

Using Optional Values:

When you have an optional value, you need to explicitly check if it's present (not `null`) before you can access the underlying value. Zig provides several ways to do this safely.

`if` **with Optional Binding:** This is a common and idiomatic way to check if an optional has a value and, if so, to create a new variable with the unwrapped value within the `if` block.

Code snippet

const std = @import("std");

```
var maybe_age: ?u32 = 30;
if (maybe_age) |age| {
    std.debug.print("Age is present: {}\n", .{age});
} else {
    std.debug.print("Age is not present (null).\n", .{});
}

maybe_age = null;
if (maybe_age) |age| {
    std.debug.print("This won't be printed.\n", .{age});
} else {
    std.debug.print("Age is now not present (null).\n", .{});
}
```

The |age| syntax within the if condition is called optional binding. If maybe_age is not null, the underlying u32 value is assigned to the new constant age within the if block's scope.

orelse **for Providing a Default Value:** If the optional is null, you can provide a default value using orelse.

Code snippet

```
var optional_count: ?usize = null;
const count = optional_count orelse 0;
std.debug.print("Count: {}\n", .{count}); // Output: Count: 0

optional_count = 10;
const actual_count = optional_count orelse 0;
std.debug.print("Actual count: {}\n", .{actual_count}); // Output:
Actual count: 10
```

Unwrapping with `.?` **(Use with Caution):** You can use the `.?` operator to unwrap an optional value directly, but this will result in a panic (program termination) at runtime if the optional is `null`. Use this only when you are absolutely certain that the optional value is present.

Code snippet

```
var definitely_has_value: ?i32 = 100;
const value = definitely_has_value.?; // Unwraps to 100

// var might_be_null: ?i32 = null;
// const will_panic = might_be_null.?; // This will cause a panic at runtime
```

Safety Benefits of Optionals:

Null Safety: Optionals force you to explicitly handle the case where a value might be absent. This prevents accidental dereferencing of null pointers, a common source of bugs in many languages.

Clarity: The ? in the type signature clearly indicates that a variable might not have a value, making the code's intent more explicit.

Compiler Assistance: The compiler helps ensure that you check for `null` before accessing the underlying value of an optional, guiding you towards writing safer code.

Combining Enums and Optionals for Complex State:

You can effectively combine enums and optionals to represent more complex states where a certain state might have associated data that could be present or absent.

Code snippet

```
const std = @import("std");

const OperationResult = enum {
    Success,
    Failure,
    Pending,
};

const UserData = struct {
    name: []const u8,
    email: ?[]const u8, // Email is optional
    status: OperationResult,
};

pub fn processUser(data: UserData) void {
    std.debug.print("User: {}\n", .{data.name});
    if (data.email) |email| {
        std.debug.print("Email: {}\n", .{email});
    } else {
        std.debug.print("Email not provided.\n", .{});
    }

    switch (data.status) {
        .Success => std.debug.print("Status: Success\n", .{}),
```

```zig
        .Failure => std.debug.print("Status: Failure\n", .{}),
        .Pending => std.debug.print("Status: Pending...\n", .{}),
    }
}

pub fn main() !void {
    const user1 = UserData{ .name = "Alice", .email =
"alice@example.com", .status = .Success };
    const user2 = UserData{ .name = "Bob", .email = null, .status =
.Pending };

    processUser(user1);
    processUser(user2);
}
```

In this example, the `UserData` struct uses an enum `OperationResult` for the status and an optional `?[]const u8` for the email, indicating that a user might not have an email address.

By leveraging enums for defining distinct states and optionals for handling the potential absence of values, Zig provides powerful tools for writing code that is both expressive and safe, reducing the likelihood of common programming errors and making your state management more explicit and robust.

CHAPTER 5

Pointers and Low-Level Programming in Zig

5.1 Working with Pointers: Dereferencing, Arithmetic, and Safety

Alright, let's tackle the topic of **Working with Pointers: Dereferencing, Arithmetic, and Safety** in Zig. Pointers are fundamental to low-level programming and allow you to directly interact with memory addresses. Zig provides powerful pointer capabilities while also incorporating safety features to help prevent common pointer-related errors.

1. What is a Pointer?

At its core, a pointer is a variable that holds the memory address of another value. Instead of containing the value itself, it "points to" where that value is stored in memory.

2. Pointer Types in Zig:

Zig has several types of pointers, each with slightly different semantics and safety implications:

*T: A pointer to a single value of type T. This is the most basic pointer type.

[*]T: A pointer to a slice of values of type T. It represents a pointer to the beginning of a contiguous block of memory containing zero or more elements of type T. The length is not part of the pointer type itself.

[N]T: A pointer to an array of N elements of type T. The size of the array is known at compile time and is part of the pointer type.

*const T: A pointer to a constant value of type T. The value being pointed to cannot be modified through this pointer.

*volatile T: A pointer to a volatile value of type T. Accesses through a volatile pointer are never optimized away and are guaranteed to have side effects. This is important for interacting with hardware or memory-mapped I/O.

*align(N) T: A pointer to a value of type T that is guaranteed to be aligned to at least N bytes in memory. Alignment is important for performance, especially when dealing with SIMD operations or hardware requirements.

3. Obtaining Pointers (Address-of Operator &):

You can get the memory address of a variable using the address-of operator &.

Code snippet

```
const std = @import("std");

pub fn main() !void {
    var age: i32 = 30;
    const age_ptr: *i32 = &age; // 'age_ptr' now holds the memory address of 'age'

    var numbers: [3]i32 = .{10, 20, 30};
    const numbers_ptr: *[3]i32 = &numbers; // Pointer to the entire array
```

```zig
    const first_element_ptr: *i32 = &numbers[0]; // Pointer to the first
element

    std.debug.print("Address of age: {}\n", .{age_ptr});
    std.debug.print("Address of numbers: {}\n", .{numbers_ptr});
            std.debug.print("Address   of   first   element:   {}\n",
.{first_element_ptr});
}
```

4. Dereferencing Pointers (The .* Operator):

To access the value that a pointer points to, you need to **dereference** it using the .* operator (pointer-dot).

Code snippet

```zig
const std = @import("std");

pub fn main() !void {
    var score: i32 = 95;
    const score_ptr: *i32 = &score;

    std.debug.print("Value of score: {}\n", .{score});      // Accessing
the value directly
        std.debug.print("Value   pointed   to   by   score_ptr:   {}\n",
.{score_ptr.*}); // Dereferencing the pointer

    score_ptr.* = 100; // Modifying the value through the pointer
    std.debug.print("Updated value of score: {}\n", .{score}); // The
original variable is changed
}
```

5. Pointer Arithmetic:

Pointer arithmetic involves performing mathematical operations on pointers. This is often used to navigate through arrays or contiguous blocks of memory.

Adding or Subtracting an Integer: Adding an integer n to a pointer of type *T advances the pointer by n * @sizeOf(T) bytes in memory. Similarly, subtracting an integer moves it backward.

Code snippet

```
const std = @import("std");

pub fn main() !void {
    var data: [5]u16 = .{100, 101, 102, 103, 104};
    const ptr: *u16 = &data[0];

    std.debug.print("First element: {}\n", .{ptr.*});       // 100
    std.debug.print("Second element: {}\n", .{(ptr + 1).*}); // 101
(moved by 1 * @sizeOf(u16) = 2 bytes)
    std.debug.print("Third element: {}\n", .{(ptr + 2).*});  // 102

    const last_ptr: *u16 = &data[4];
    std.debug.print("Last element: {}\n", .{last_ptr.*});     // 104
    std.debug.print("Second to last: {}\n", .{(last_ptr - 1).*}); // 103
}
```

Subtracting Two Pointers: Subtracting one pointer from another (of the same type) yields the number of elements of that type between the two addresses.

Code snippet

```
const std = @import("std");
```

```
pub fn main() !void {
    var values: [5]i32 = .{1, 2, 3, 4, 5};
    const start: *i32 = &values[0];
    const end: *i32 = &values[4];

    const distance = end - start; // Result is 4 (number of i32
elements)
    std.debug.print("Distance between pointers: {}\n", .{distance});
}
```

Important Note on Pointer Arithmetic Safety: Zig allows pointer arithmetic, but it's crucial to perform it within the bounds of allocated memory. Going beyond the allocated region can lead to undefined behavior and crashes. Zig's slice pointers ([*]T) often provide a safer way to work with contiguous memory as they carry size information.

6. Pointer Safety in Zig:

Zig incorporates several features to enhance pointer safety compared to languages like C and C++:

Explicit Pointer Types: The distinction between raw pointers (*T), slice pointers ([*]T), and array pointers (*[N]T) helps the compiler understand the intended use and potential bounds.

Bounds Checking (in Debug Builds): In debug builds, Zig often performs bounds checks on array and slice accesses, which can help catch out-of-bounds pointer dereferences.

Optional Pointers (?*T): Pointers can also be optional, indicating that they might be null. You need to explicitly check for null before dereferencing an optional pointer, similar to other optional types.

Code snippet

```
const std = @import("std");

pub fn main() !void {
    var maybe_ptr: ?*i32 = null;

    // if (maybe_ptr) |ptr| { // Safe way to dereference
    //     std.debug.print("Value: {}\n", .{ptr.*});
    // } else {
    //     std.debug.print("Pointer is null.\n", .{});
    // }

    // maybe_ptr.* = 10; // This would cause a panic if maybe_ptr is null

    var value = 42;
    maybe_ptr = &value;
    if (maybe_ptr) |ptr| {
        std.debug.print("Value: {}\n", .{ptr.*}); // Now it's safe
    }
}
```

Pointer Provenance (Ongoing Development): Zig is actively developing features related to pointer provenance, which aims to track the origin and validity of pointers more rigorously at compile time, further enhancing memory safety.

7. Common Use Cases for Pointers:

Passing Data by Reference: Pointers allow functions to modify the original data passed to them without making a copy, which can be more efficient for large data structures.

Working with Dynamic Memory: When you allocate memory on the heap, you receive a pointer to the beginning of the allocated block.

Interfacing with Hardware: Low-level hardware interaction often involves reading from and writing to specific memory addresses using pointers.

Data Structures: Many advanced data structures (like linked lists, trees) rely heavily on pointers to link their elements.

Interoperability with C: C relies heavily on pointers, so understanding them is crucial for Zig's excellent C interoperability.

Important Considerations for Pointer Safety:

Avoid Dangling Pointers: Ensure that you do not dereference pointers that point to memory that has been deallocated.

Stay Within Bounds: When performing pointer arithmetic on arrays or slices, always ensure you are within the valid memory region.

Handle Null Pointers: If you are working with optional pointers or pointers that could potentially be `null`, always check for `null` before dereferencing.

Be Mindful of Mutability: Use `*const T` when you want to ensure that the data being pointed to is not modified through that pointer.

Working with pointers in Zig provides a lot of power and control, but it also requires careful attention to memory management and safety. By understanding the different pointer types, how to dereference them, and the safety features Zig offers, you can leverage pointers effectively while minimizing the risk of common pointer-related errors.

5.2 Interacting with Raw Memory: Slices and Arrays in Depth

Alright, let's delve into **Interacting with Raw Memory: Slices and Arrays in Depth** within Zig. Understanding how these fundamental data structures relate to memory is crucial for efficient and safe programming, especially when dealing with low-level operations or performance-critical code.

1. Arrays: Contiguous Blocks of Fixed Size

Memory Layout: An array in Zig (declared as $[N]T$) represents a contiguous block of N elements of type T in memory. The elements are stored one after another, with no gaps (unless padding is added by the compiler for alignment). The size of the array is fixed at compile time and is part of its type.

Stack vs. Heap Allocation: Arrays can be allocated on the stack if they are local variables within a function and their size is known at compile time. They can also be part of structs or unions, which themselves might be on the stack or heap. For dynamic sizing or when the array needs to outlive the current scope, you would typically allocate memory on the heap and then potentially use an array pointer or slice to interact with it.

Accessing Elements: You access individual elements of an array using the index operator $[]$, where the index is a usize (unsigned size type) starting from 0.

Code snippet

```zig
const std = @import("std");

pub fn main() !void {
    var numbers: [5]i32 = .{10, 20, 30, 40, 50};
    std.debug.print("First element: {}\n", .{numbers[0]}); // Accessing
the element at index 0
    numbers[2] = 35; // Modifying the element at index 2
    std.debug.print("Updated array: {}\n", .{numbers});
}
```

Safety: Zig performs bounds checking on array access in debug builds. If you try to access an element outside the valid range (0 to N-1), it will result in a runtime panic. In release builds, bounds checking might be omitted for performance, so it's crucial to ensure your indices are within bounds.

Pointers to Arrays: You can obtain a pointer to the beginning of an array using the & operator. The type of this pointer will be *[N]T.

Code snippet

```zig
const data: [3]u8 = .{1, 2, 3};
const ptr_to_array: *[3]u8 = &data;
std.debug.print("Pointer to array: {}\n", .{ptr_to_array});
std.debug.print("First element via pointer: {}\n", .{ptr_to_array[0]});
// You can still use index access on array pointers
```

2. Slices: Dynamically-Sized Views into Memory

Concept: A slice in Zig (declared as [ ] T) is a dynamically-sized view into a contiguous sequence of elements of type T in memory. A slice consists of two parts: a pointer to the first element of the sequence and a length (the number of elements in the view).

Memory Ownership: A slice does *not* own the underlying memory. It's just a reference to a part of some other memory (which could be an array, a heap allocation, or even memory-mapped I/O). This is a crucial distinction from arrays, which own their data.

Creating Slices: You can create slices from arrays or from pointers and a length.

From an array:

Code snippet

```
const numbers: [5]i32 = .{10, 20, 30, 40, 50};
const slice_of_numbers: []const i32 = numbers[1..4]; // Creates a slice from index 1 up to (but not including) 4
std.debug.print("Slice: {}\n", .{slice_of_numbers}); // Output: &[20, 30, 40]
std.debug.print("Length of slice: {}\n", .{slice_of_numbers.len}); // Output: 3
```

From a pointer and a length:

Code snippet

```
const std = @import("std");

pub fn main() !void {
    const allocator = std.heap.GeneralPurposeAllocator.init(std.heap.page_allocator){}.allocator();
    defer std.heap.GeneralPurposeAllocator.deinit(allocator);

    const count: usize = 10;
    const buffer = try allocator.alloc(u8, count);
    defer allocator.free(buffer, count);

    for (0..count) |i| {
        buffer[i] = @intCast(u8, i * 10);
    }

    const byte_slice: []u8 = buffer[0..count];
    std.debug.print("Byte slice: {}\n", .{byte_slice});
    std.debug.print("Length of byte slice: {}\n", .{byte_slice.len}); // Output: 10
}
```

Accessing Elements: You access elements of a slice using the index operator [ ], just like with arrays.

Code snippet

```
const data: [5]i32 = .{1, 2, 3, 4, 5};
const slice: []const i32 = data[1..]; // Slice from index 1 to the end
std.debug.print("Second element of slice: {}\n", .{slice[0]}); // Corresponds to data[1]
```

Safety: Similar to arrays, Zig performs bounds checking on slice access in debug builds. Accessing an index outside the slice's length will cause a panic.

Mutability: Slices themselves are just views. Whether you can modify the elements of a slice depends on the mutability of the underlying memory it refers to. If the slice is created from a var array or a mutable heap allocation, and the slice is also declared as var or without const, you can modify the elements through the slice.

Code snippet

```
const std = @import("std");

pub fn main() !void {
    var numbers: [3]i32 = .{1, 2, 3};
```

```
    var mutable_slice: []i32 = numbers[0..2];
    mutable_slice[0] = 100;
    std.debug.print("Modified slice: {}\n", .{mutable_slice}); // Output:
&[100, 2]
    std.debug.print("Original array: {}\n", .{numbers});    // Output:
&[100, 2, 3] (original array is also modified)
}
```

3. Interacting with Raw Memory using Pointers and Slices:

Slices are often used as a safe and convenient way to interact with raw memory pointed to by a pointer. Since a slice carries both the starting address and the length, it helps prevent out-of-bounds accesses.

Code snippet

```
const std = @import("std");

pub fn main() !void {
    const allocator =
std.heap.GeneralPurposeAllocator.init(std.heap.page_allocator){}.
allocator();
    defer std.heap.GeneralPurposeAllocator.deinit(allocator);

    const size: usize = 256;
    const raw_memory = try allocator.alloc(u8, size);
    defer allocator.free(raw_memory, size);

    // Create a slice view of this raw memory
    const byte_slice: []u8 = raw_memory[0..size];
```

```zig
// Initialize the memory using the slice
for (byte_slice, i) |*byte, index| {
    byte.* = @intCast(u8, index % 256);
}

// Print a portion of the memory through the slice
    std.debug.print("First 32 bytes of raw memory: {}\n",
.{byte_slice[0..32]});

// You can also create a slice of a different type over the same
raw memory
    const as_i32_slice: []i32 = @as([*]i32, @ptrCast([*]u8,
raw_memory))[0..size / @sizeOf(i32)];
    std.debug.print("First few i32 values: {}\n", .{as_i32_slice[0..8]});
}
```

Key Concepts:

Contiguous Memory: Both arrays and the underlying memory of slices are contiguous blocks in memory.

Fixed vs. Dynamic Size: Arrays have a fixed size known at compile time, while slices have a dynamic length determined at runtime.

Ownership: Arrays own their data, while slices are just views into memory owned elsewhere.

Safety through Bounds Checking: Zig provides bounds checking for both array and slice access in debug builds.

Flexibility of Slices: Slices are very flexible for working with portions of arrays or dynamically allocated memory.

Type Casting for Raw Memory: You can use `@as` and `@ptrCast` to reinterpret raw memory (accessed via a `[*]u8` slice or pointer) as a slice of a different type, but you need to be very careful about alignment and size.

Use Cases:

Working with Buffers: Slices are commonly used to represent buffers of data, such as those read from files or network sockets.

Iterating over Collections: Slices provide a convenient way to iterate over elements of arrays or dynamic data.

Passing Subsets of Data: You can easily pass a portion of an array to a function by creating a slice.

Low-Level Operations: When dealing with raw memory allocated on the heap or when interacting with external systems, slices provide a safe way to manage the memory region.

Understanding the relationship between arrays, slices, and raw memory is fundamental for effective memory manipulation in Zig. Slices, in particular, offer a powerful and often safer way to work with contiguous memory regions of dynamic size.

5.3 System Calls and Interfacing with the Operating System (Basics)

Alright, let's touch upon the basics of **System Calls and Interfacing with the Operating System (OS)** in Zig. While Zig aims to be a high-performance language with a small runtime, interacting with the underlying OS is often necessary for tasks like file I/O, networking, process management, and more.

1. What are System Calls?

A system call is a request made by a user-level program to the operating system kernel to perform a privileged operation. The kernel has direct access to the system's hardware and resources, and system calls provide a controlled and secure way for applications to interact with these resources.

Think of it like this: your Zig program is a regular citizen in a city (the operating system). To do something important like opening a bank vault (accessing a file on disk) or talking to someone in another city (using network sockets), you need to go through the city's authorities (the kernel) and make a formal request (a system call).

2. How Zig Interacts with the OS:

Zig, being a systems programming language, provides mechanisms to make system calls. These mechanisms are typically exposed through its standard library (std). The standard library wraps the raw system calls in a more type-safe and convenient API.

Directly making raw system calls can be platform-specific and error-prone. The std library aims to provide a more portable and safer interface.

3. Examples of OS Interaction through std:

Let's look at some basic examples of how a Zig program can interact with the OS using the standard library:

File I/O (Reading a File):

Code snippet

```
const std = @import("std");
```

```
const fs = std.fs;

pub fn main() !void {
    const file_path = "my_file.txt";

    // Open the file for reading
    const file = try fs.openFile(file_path, .{}, 0);
    defer file.close();

    // Get the size of the file
    const file_info = try file.stat();
    const file_size = file_info.size;

    // Allocate a buffer to read the file contents
    const buffer = try std.heap.page_allocator.alloc(u8, file_size);
    defer std.heap.page_allocator.free(buffer, file_size);

    // Read the entire file into the buffer
    const bytes_read = try file.read(buffer);
        std.debug.print("Read {} bytes from {}:\n{}\n", .{bytes_read,
file_path, buffer[0..bytes_read]});
}
```

In this example, `fs.openFile`, `file.stat`, `std.heap.page_allocator.alloc`, `file.read`, and `file.close` are all functions in the standard library that internally make system calls to interact with the file system.

Printing to Standard Output:

We've already seen this with `std.debug.print`. This function ultimately uses system calls to write data to the standard output stream (usually your terminal).

Exiting the Program:

Code snippet

```
const std = @import("std");
const os = std.os;

pub fn main() !void {
    std.debug.print("Program starting...\n", .{});
    // ... some operations ...
    os.exit(0); // Exit the program with an exit code of 0 (success)
}
```

`os.exit()` makes a system call to terminate the current process.

Getting the Current Time (More involved, platform-specific details abstracted by `std`):

Code snippet

```
const std = @import("std");
const time = std.time;

pub fn main() !void {
    const now = time.now();
```

```
    std.debug.print("Current time (raw): {}\n", .{now});
    // Formatting the time into a human-readable format would
involve more steps.
}
```

`time.now()` internally uses system calls to query the system's clock.

4. Abstraction and Portability:

The Zig standard library provides a level of abstraction over the underlying operating system. This means that code written using the `std` APIs is often more portable across different operating systems (like Linux, Windows, macOS) because the library handles the platform-specific details of the system calls.

However, there are still cases where you might need to write platform-specific code or interact with OS-specific features that are not abstracted by the standard library. Zig provides ways to do this as well, often involving importing OS-specific modules or even making raw syscalls (though this is less common and requires more care).

5. Error Handling:

Interacting with the OS can often lead to errors (e.g., file not found, permission denied, network connection failed). The standard library functions that perform OS operations typically return error unions (using the `!` syntax), requiring you to handle these potential errors using `try` and `catch`.

6. Low-Level OS Interaction (Beyond `std` - Advanced Topic):

While the standard library covers many common OS interactions, Zig also allows for more direct interaction if needed. This might involve:

Importing OS-Specific Modules: Zig might provide modules (e.g., `std.os.linux`, `std.os.windows`) that expose more OS-specific APIs.

Making Raw System Calls (Advanced and Unsafe): In very specific scenarios, you might need to make raw system calls directly. This is highly platform-dependent and generally requires a deep understanding of the target OS's system call interface. It also often involves using Zig's `@syscall` builtin, which bypasses the standard library's safety checks and portability layers. This should be done with extreme caution.

In summary, interacting with the operating system is a fundamental aspect of many programs. Zig's standard library provides a relatively high-level, type-safe, and portable way to perform common OS operations like file I/O, process management, and networking. It abstracts away many of the platform-specific details of system calls and provides error handling mechanisms. While Zig also allows for more direct and low-level OS interaction, this is typically reserved for advanced use cases where fine-grained control or access to OS-specific features is required.

As you build more complex applications in Zig, you'll inevitably use the standard library to interact with the underlying operating system to perform various tasks. Understanding this interaction is key to building real-world applications.

CHAPTER 6

Concurrency and Asynchronous Operations

6.1 Understanding Concurrency Models in Zig (async/await)

Alright, let's explore **Understanding Concurrency Models in Zig, specifically focusing on** async/await. Concurrency allows your program to perform multiple tasks seemingly at the same time, improving responsiveness and efficiency, especially in I/O-bound operations. Zig's approach to concurrency through async/await is designed to be efficient, explicit, and integrated deeply into the language.

1. What is Concurrency?

Concurrency is the ability of a program to work on multiple tasks within the same time period. This doesn't necessarily mean those tasks are executing *at the exact same instant* (that's parallelism, which often involves multiple CPU cores). Instead, a concurrent program can switch between tasks, making progress on each without waiting for one to complete fully before starting another.

2. Asynchronous Operations and async/await:

The async/await model is a popular way to handle concurrency, particularly for I/O-bound operations (like network requests, file reading/writing) where waiting for the operation to complete can block the entire program.

async **Functions:** An async function in Zig (declared with the async fn syntax) is a special kind of function that, when called, doesn't execute immediately to completion. Instead, it returns a special object called a `Task`. This `Task` represents the ongoing computation of the asynchronous function.

`await` **Operator:** The `await` operator is used within an `async` function to pause the execution of that function until the `Task` it's awaiting on has completed and produced a result (or an error). While the `async` function is paused, the underlying concurrency mechanism can allow other `Task`s to make progress. Once the awaited `Task` finishes, the `async` function resumes execution from where it left off.

3. Zig's `async`/`await` **Implementation:**

Zig's `async`/`await` is built into the language and is designed with efficiency and explicitness in mind. Here are some key aspects:

No Implicit Threading: Zig's `async`/`await` itself doesn't automatically spawn new threads. It provides the *mechanism* for asynchronous operations, but you, the programmer, are responsible for providing the **executor** that will run these `Task`s. This explicitness gives you more control over how your concurrent code is executed (e.g., using a single thread with an event loop, a thread pool, or a custom scheduler).

`Task` **Type:** The `async fn` returns a `Task(return_type)`. This `Task` is a lightweight representation of the asynchronous computation. It's similar to a promise or a future in other languages.

Integration with Error Handling: Asynchronous functions can also return errors using the `!` syntax (e.g., `async fn` `fetchData()  ![]u8)`. When you `await` a `Task` that can return an error, you can use `try` to propagate the error.

4. Basic Example (Conceptual - Requires an Executor):

Code snippet

```
const std = @import("std");
const time = std.time;

async fn fetchData(url: []const u8) ![]u8 {
    std.debug.print("Fetching data from {}...\n", .{url});
        await time.sleep(time.milliseconds(100)); // Simulate an asynchronous I/O operation
    std.debug.print("Data fetched from {}.\n", .{url});
     return "Data from URL"; // In a real scenario, this would be the fetched data
}

async fn processData(data: []const u8) void {
    std.debug.print("Processing data: {}\n", .{data});
    await time.sleep(time.milliseconds(50));
    std.debug.print("Data processed.\n", .{data});
}

pub fn main() !void {
    // In a real application, you would need to set up an executor
    // to run these tasks concurrently. For this conceptual example,
    // we'll just illustrate the async/await syntax.

    const task1 = fetchData("example.com/data1");
    const task2 = fetchData("example.com/data2");

    // To actually run these concurrently, you would typically submit them
```

```
// to an executor and then await their completion.

// For a sequential (non-concurrent) execution for illustration:
const result1 = try await task1;
std.debug.print("Result 1: {}\n", .{result1});

const result2 = try await task2;
std.debug.print("Result 2: {}\n", .{result2});

await processData(result1);
await processData(result2);
}
```

Important Note: The `main` function in the example above is synchronous. To truly leverage the concurrency of `async/await`, you would typically have an `async main` function (if the runtime environment supports it) or, more commonly, you would create an executor (like an event loop or a thread pool) and submit the `Task`s to it.

5. Executors (The Missing Piece in the Basic Example):

An **executor** is responsible for taking `Task`s and running them. It manages the underlying mechanisms (e.g., a single thread with non-blocking I/O, multiple threads) to achieve concurrency.

Zig's standard library provides some tools for building executors, such as `std.async.EventLoop`, but setting up a full-fledged executor can be more involved and depends on the specific concurrency needs of your application.

6. Benefits of `async/await` in Zig:

Improved Responsiveness: For I/O-bound operations, `async/await` allows your program to remain responsive by not blocking the main thread while waiting for I/O to complete.

Structured Concurrency: It provides a more structured and easier-to-reason-about way to write concurrent code compared to traditional callbacks or raw threading. The `async/await` syntax makes asynchronous code look more like synchronous code, improving readability.

Efficiency: By allowing the program to switch between tasks while waiting for I/O, it can make better use of system resources.

Explicitness: Zig's design keeps the concurrency model explicit. You are aware that a function is asynchronous because of the `async` keyword, and you explicitly use `await` to pause execution. The lack of a built-in implicit executor gives you more control.

7. Considerations and Challenges:

Executor Implementation: You need to either use an existing executor (if provided by a library or framework) or implement your own, which can be complex.

Asynchronous Ecosystem: The ecosystem of asynchronous libraries might be less mature in Zig compared to languages with built-in concurrency models and large standard libraries.

Learning Curve: Understanding how `async/await` works and how to use executors effectively requires a learning curve.

In summary, Zig's `async/await` provides a powerful and efficient way to write concurrent code, particularly for I/O-bound operations. It allows you to define asynchronous functions that return `Task`s, and you can use `await` to pause execution until a `Task` completes. However, it's important to remember that Zig's `async/await` doesn't include a built-in executor, so you need to provide one to actually run these tasks concurrently.

As Zig evolves, we might see more standardized executors or libraries that provide them, making it easier to leverage the `async/await` features. For now, understanding the core mechanism is the first step.

6.2 Working with Goroutines (or Zig's equivalent) and Synchronization Primitives

You're thinking about concurrency, and you're drawing a parallel to Go's Goroutines! That's a great way to frame it. While Zig doesn't have a direct feature named "Goroutines," it achieves similar concurrency capabilities through its `async/await` mechanism, which we just discussed, and by leveraging **lightweight threads** or **fibers** that can be managed by an executor.

Let's break down how you'd achieve something similar to Goroutines in Zig and the synchronization primitives you'd use:

1. Zig's Equivalent of "Starting a Goroutine":

In Zig, you would typically "start" a concurrent task by calling an `async` function. This call returns a `Task`, which represents the asynchronous operation. To actually run this task concurrently, you need to submit it to an **executor**.

Think of it this way:

`async fn myTask()` ...: This defines a piece of work that *can* run concurrently (like a Goroutine function).

`const task = myTask();` : This *creates* a representation of that work (the `Task`), but it doesn't necessarily start running immediately or in a new thread.

Submitting the `task` to an executor: This is the step that schedules the `Task` to be executed concurrently, often managed by an event loop or a thread pool.

Example (Conceptual with a Hypothetical Executor):

Code snippet

```
const std = @import("std");
const time = std.time;
const assert = std.debug.assert;

async fn worker(id: u32, counter: *std.atomic.Usize) !void {
    std.debug.print("[Worker {}]: Starting...\n", .{id});
    await time.sleep(time.milliseconds(@as(u64, id) * 50));
    counter.fetchAdd(1, .Monotonic);
        std.debug.print("[Worker {}]: Finished. Counter: {}\n", .{id,
counter.load(.Monotonic)});
}

pub fn main() !void {
    const num_workers: u32 = 5;
    var counter = std.atomic.Usize.init(0);

    // Hypothetical executor (not part of std yet in this form)
    const executor = std.async.EventLoop.init();
    defer executor.deinit();

    var tasks: [num_workers]?std.async.Task(void) = undefined;

    // Launch "Goroutine-like" tasks
```

```
for (0..num_workers) |i| {
    tasks[i] = executor.spawn(worker(i, &counter));
}

// Wait for all tasks to complete (again, executor-specific)
for (tasks) |maybe_task| {
    if (maybe_task) |task| {
        try await task;
    }
}

assert(counter.load(.Monotonic) == num_workers);
    std.debug.print("All workers finished. Final counter: {}\n",
.{counter.load(.Monotonic)});
}
```

In this conceptual example, `executor.spawn(worker(...))` is akin to `go worker(...)` in Go. It schedules the `async` function `worker` to run concurrently.

2. Synchronization Primitives in Zig:

When you have concurrent tasks accessing shared resources, you need synchronization primitives to prevent race conditions and ensure data consistency. Zig provides several tools for this in the `std.sync` module:

`std.atomic` **Types:** These provide atomic operations on primitive types (like integers and booleans). Atomic operations are guaranteed to be indivisible and are essential for low-level synchronization without explicit locks in simple cases.

Code snippet

```
const std = @import("std");
const time = std.time;

async fn incrementer(counter: *std.atomic.Usize) !void {
    for (0..1000) |_| {
        counter.fetchAdd(1, .Monotonic);
        await time.sleep(time.microseconds(1));
    }
}

pub fn main() !void {
    var shared_counter = std.atomic.Usize.init(0);
    const num_increments = 2;
    var tasks: [num_increments]?std.async.Task(void) = undefined;
    const executor = std.async.EventLoop.init();
    defer executor.deinit();

    for (0..num_increments) |i| {
        tasks[i] = executor.spawn(incrementer(&shared_counter));
    }

    for (tasks) |maybe_task| {
        if (maybe_task) |task| {
            try await task;
        }
    }

    std.debug.print("Final     counter     value:     {}\n",
.{shared_counter.load(.Monotonic)});
    // The final value should be 2000 (1000 increments from each
task).
}
```

`std.sync.Mutex` **(Mutual Exclusion Lock):** A mutex protects a shared resource by allowing only one task to hold the lock at a time. Other tasks trying to access the locked resource will block until the lock is released.

Code snippet

```
const std = @import("std");
const time = std.time;
const sync = std.sync;

var shared_data: i32 = 0;
var mutex = sync.Mutex{};

async fn modify_data(id: u32) !void {
    mutex.lock();
    defer mutex.unlock();
    std.debug.print("[Task {}]: Acquired lock. Shared data was: {}\n", .{id, shared_data});
    shared_data += 1;
    await time.sleep(time.milliseconds(10));
    std.debug.print("[Task {}]: Released lock. Shared data is now: {}\n", .{id, shared_data});
}

pub fn main() !void {
    const num_tasks = 3;
    var tasks: [num_tasks]?std.async.Task(void) = undefined;
    const executor = std.async.EventLoop.init();
    defer executor.deinit();
```

```
for (0..num_tasks) |i| {
    tasks[i] = executor.spawn(modify_data(@as(u32, i)));
}

for (tasks) |maybe_task| {
    if (maybe_task) |task| {
        try await task;
    }
}

    std.debug.print("Final shared data value: {}\n", .{shared_data});
// Should be 3
}
```

std.sync.RwLock **(Read-Write Lock):** A read-write lock allows multiple readers to access a shared resource concurrently but requires exclusive access for writers.[1] This can improve performance when reads are much more frequent than writes.

Code snippet

```
// (Conceptual example - usage would be similar to Mutex with
.readLock() and .writeLock())
```

`std.sync.Semaphore`: A semaphore is a signaling mechanism that can control access to a limited number of resources. It maintains a counter that is incremented by `acquire()` (if the counter is greater than zero) and decremented by `release()`.

Code snippet

// (Conceptual example - useful for limiting concurrent access to a pool of resources)

`std.sync.CondVar` **(Condition Variable):** Condition variables are used in conjunction with mutexes to allow tasks to wait for a specific condition to become true. A task acquires a mutex, checks the condition, and if it's false, waits on the condition variable. Another task that changes the condition signals the waiting task.

Code snippet

// (More complex primitive for coordinating tasks based on conditions)

Key Differences from Go's Goroutines:

Explicit Executors: In Zig, you generally need to explicitly create and manage an executor to run `async` tasks concurrently. Go has a built-in scheduler for Goroutines.

Language-Level Integration: Goroutines and the `go` keyword are more deeply integrated into Go's syntax. Zig's `async/await` is also a language feature, but the execution model is more explicit.

Standard Library Maturity: Go's concurrency primitives and standard library support for concurrency are more mature and extensive at this point. Zig's `async/await` is still evolving.

In summary, while Zig doesn't have "Goroutines" by name, you achieve similar concurrency using `async` functions and by running the resulting `Task`s on an executor (like an event loop). For synchronizing concurrent access to shared resources, Zig provides a range of primitives in `std.sync`, including atomics, mutexes, read-write locks, semaphores, and condition variables. The key difference is the more explicit nature of executor management in Zig compared to Go's built-in scheduler.

6.3 Building Responsive Applications with Asynchronous Programming

You're spot on! Building responsive applications is a prime use case for asynchronous programming, and Zig's `async/await` features are well-suited for this purpose. Let's explore how asynchronous programming in Zig helps in creating responsive applications, especially in the context of I/O-bound operations that can otherwise lead to blocking and a frozen user interface.

Why Asynchronous Programming for Responsiveness?

In many applications, especially those that interact with external resources like networks, filesystems, or databases, a significant portion of the application's runtime can be spent waiting for these operations to complete. If these operations are performed synchronously (blocking), the entire application's main thread (often responsible for the user interface) will freeze, leading to a poor user experience.

Asynchronous programming allows these potentially long-running operations to be initiated without blocking the main thread. When the operation completes, a notification or callback mechanism is used to resume the relevant part of the application's logic. This keeps the main thread free to handle user interactions and update the UI, resulting in a more responsive application.

How Zig's async/await **Contributes to Responsiveness:**

1.**Non-Blocking Operations:** When you await an async function in Zig that performs an I/O operation (assuming the underlying I/O is implemented non-blocking), the current async function will yield control back to the executor. This prevents the current thread (which might be the UI thread) from being blocked while waiting for the I/O to finish.

2. **Event Loops and Executors:** To truly achieve responsiveness, you need an executor, often an event loop, that can manage multiple Tasks. The event loop monitors the status of asynchronous operations. When an operation completes (e.g., data arrives from a network socket, a file is read), the event loop can schedule the continuation of the corresponding async function.

3. **Maintaining UI Thread Responsiveness:** In UI applications, the main thread is typically responsible for handling user input, rendering the UI, and responding to events. By performing I/O-bound tasks asynchronously and using an executor that doesn't block the main UI thread, you can ensure that the UI

remains interactive even when the application is busy with background operations.

Conceptual Example (UI Application with Asynchronous Networking):

Imagine a simple application that fetches data from a remote API and displays it in the UI.

Code snippet

```
const std = @import("std");
const http = std.http;
const uri = std.uri;
const json = std.json;
const time = std.time;

// Assume we have a UI framework (not part of std) that provides
// a main event loop and a way to update the UI.

async fn fetchUserData(url: []const u8, ui_context: *UIContext) !void {
    std.debug.print("[Fetch]: Starting request to {}\n", .{url});
    const client = http.Client{}; // Assume a non-blocking HTTP client
    defer client.deinit();

    const parsed_uri = try uri.parse(url);
    const response = try await client.get(parsed_uri, .{});
    defer response.deinit();

    if (response.status != .OK) {
        std.debug.print("[Fetch]: Error - Status {}\n", .{response.status});
        ui_context.updateStatus("Error fetching data");
```

```zig
        return;
    }

    const body = try await response.readBodyAlloc(std.heap.page_allocator, 4096);
    defer std.heap.page_allocator.free(body);

    std.debug.print("[Fetch]: Received data: {}\n", .{body});

    // Parse the JSON data (assuming the API returns JSON)
    var parser = json.Parser.init(body);
    const userData = try parser.parseValue(json.Value);

    // Update the UI with the fetched data (this would need to
interact with the UI framework)
    ui_context.updateUserData(userData);
    ui_context.updateStatus("Data loaded successfully");
}

// Hypothetical UI Context
const UIContext = struct {
    pub fn updateUserData(self: *UIContext, data: any) void {
        std.debug.print("[UI]: Updating UI with data: {}\n", .{data});
        // Code to actually update UI elements would go here
    }

    pub fn updateStatus(self: *UIContext, status: []const u8) void {
        std.debug.print("[UI]: Status: {}\n", .{status});
        // Code to update a status label in the UI
    }
};

pub fn main() !void {
    var ui_context = UIContext{};
```

```
    // When a button is clicked in the UI, we might start the data
fetch
    const data_url = "https://api.example.com/users/1";
    const fetch_task = fetchUserData(data_url, &ui_context);

    // To actually run this without blocking the UI, 'fetch_task' would
need
    // to be submitted to the UI framework's event loop or an
asynchronous executor
    // that integrates with the UI.

    // In a simplified, non-UI context, you might use something like:
    const executor = std.async.EventLoop.init();
    defer executor.deinit();
    executor.spawn(fetch_task);

    // The UI event loop would continue to run here, handling user
input
    // and updating the UI while 'fetchUserData' is running in the
background.

    // For this simple example, we'll just sleep to simulate the UI
running
    await time.sleep(time.seconds(5));
    std.debug.print("UI still responsive...\n", .{});
}
```

Key Principles for Responsive Applications with
`async`/`await`:

1.**Identify Blocking Operations:** Pinpoint the parts of your application that perform I/O or other potentially long-running tasks.

2. **Use** `async` **for I/O-Bound Functions:** Make functions that initiate these operations `async`.

3. `await` **the Results:** Use `await` to pause the execution of the `async` function until the result is available, but this should not block the main UI thread if you're using a proper asynchronous executor.

4. **Integrate with an Event Loop or Executor:** You need a mechanism (provided by a UI framework or a custom executor) to manage the execution of these `async` tasks and to handle their completion. This executor should be non-blocking with respect to the UI thread.

5. **Update UI on the Main Thread:** If your `async` tasks need to update the UI, ensure that the UI updates are performed on the main UI thread to avoid race conditions and ensure proper rendering. UI frameworks typically provide mechanisms to dispatch work back to the main thread.

Challenges in Zig (Current State):

As mentioned earlier, Zig's standard library is still evolving in its asynchronous capabilities, especially concerning UI integration. You might find that for building complex UI applications with asynchronous operations, you might need to rely on external UI frameworks (which might have their own concurrency models) or build more of the asynchronous infrastructure yourself using Zig's primitives.

In conclusion, Zig's `async`/`await` provides the foundation for building responsive applications by allowing you to perform potentially blocking operations without freezing the main execution flow. However, achieving true responsiveness, especially in UI applications, requires the integration of these asynchronous tasks with an appropriate executor or event loop that is designed to keep the UI thread responsive. As Zig's ecosystem grows, we might see more high-level abstractions and libraries that simplify the creation of responsive applications using asynchronous programming.

CHAPTER 7

Testing and Debugging Your Zig Code

7.1 Writing Unit Tests with Zig's Built-in Testing Framework

You're right on track! Writing unit tests is crucial for ensuring the correctness and reliability of your Zig code. Zig has a built-in testing framework that makes it straightforward to define and run tests directly within your source files. Let's explore how to use it.

1. Defining Tests:

In Zig, you define unit tests within your `.zig` files using the `test` keyword followed by a descriptive name for the test case and a block of code containing the test logic.

The basic syntax for defining a test is:

Code snippet

```
test "name_of_the_test" {
    // Test logic goes here
    // Assertions to check for expected outcomes
}
```

`test`: This keyword marks the beginning of a test function.

`"name_of_the_test"`: This is a string literal that serves as the name or description of your test case. Choose names that clearly indicate what the test is verifying.

{ ... }: The curly braces enclose the body of the test function, where you'll write the code to exercise the unit under test and assert the expected behavior.

2. Assertions:

Within your test functions, you'll use assertion functions to check if the actual outcome of your code matches the expected outcome. Zig's standard library (`std.debug`) provides the `assert` function for this purpose.

Code snippet

```
const std = @import("std");
const assert = std.debug.assert;

test "addition works correctly" {
    const a = 5;
    const b = 3;
    const sum = a + b;
    assert(sum == 8); // This assertion will pass

    const x = 10;
    const y = 2;
    const product = x * y;
    assert(product == 20); // This assertion will also pass
}

test "string comparison" {
    const greeting = "Hello";
    const expected = "Hello";
    assert(std.mem.eql(u8, greeting, expected));

    const different = "World";
    assert(!std.mem.eql(u8, greeting, different));
```

}

If an assertion within a test fails (the condition evaluates to `false`), the test will be marked as failed when you run the tests.

3. Running Tests:

You can run the tests in your Zig project using the Zig compiler with the `test` subcommand:

Bash

zig test your_file.zig

If you have multiple `.zig` files in your project, you can run all the tests in the current directory and its subdirectories using:

Bash

zig test .

When you run the tests, Zig will compile your code and then execute all the functions marked with the `test` keyword. It will report the status of each test (pass or fail) along with any error messages if an assertion fails.

4. Organizing Tests:

As your project grows, you might want to organize your tests into logical groups. You can do this by having multiple `test` functions within a single file or by creating separate files specifically for tests (e.g., `your_module_test.zig`).

Code snippet

```
// math.zig
pub fn add(a: i32, b: i32) i32 {
    return a + b;
}

pub fn multiply(a: i32, b: i32) i32 {
    return a * b;
}

// math_test.zig
const std = @import("std");
const assert = std.debug.assert;
const math = @import("./math.zig");

test "math.add works" {
    assert(math.add(2, 3) == 5);
    assert(math.add(-1, 1) == 0);
    assert(math.add(0, 0) == 0);
}

test "math.multiply works" {
    assert(math.multiply(2, 3) == 6);
    assert(math.multiply(-1, 5) == -5);
    assert(math.multiply(0, 10) == 0);
}
```

To run these tests, you would use:

Bash

```
zig test math_test.zig
```

5. Testing Error Scenarios:

When testing functions that can return errors (using the ! syntax), you'll often want to assert that an error is returned under specific conditions. You can use the error type and compare the result of a try block within a catch block.

Code snippet

```
const std = @import("std");
const assert = std.debug.assert;
const fs = std.fs;

fn readFileContents(path: []const u8) ![]u8 {
    const file = try fs.openFile(path, .{}, 0);
    defer file.close();
    const contents = try std.fs.readFileAlloc(std.heap.page_allocator, file, std.math.maxInt(usize));
    return contents;
}

test "readFileContents succeeds for existing file" {
    const path = "test_file.txt";
    const expected_contents = "Test content";
    try std.fs.writeFile(path, expected_contents, .{ .create = true, .truncate = true });
    defer std.fs.deleteFile(path) catch {};

    const contents = try readFileContents(path);
    assert(std.mem.eql(u8, contents, expected_contents));
    std.heap.page_allocator.free(contents);
}

test "readFileContents returns error for non-existent file" {
    const non_existent_path = "non_existent.txt";
    const result = readFileContents(non_existent_path);
```

```
    assert(result == error.FileNotFound);
}
```

6. Test-Driven Development (TDD):

Zig's built-in testing framework encourages a TDD approach where you write tests *before* you write the actual implementation code. This helps you clarify the requirements and design of your functions and modules.

7. Benefits of Using Zig's Testing Framework:

Built-in: No need for external dependencies or test runners.

Simple Syntax: Easy to define and run tests.

Integration: Tests live alongside your code, making it easy to find and update them.

Clear Reporting: Provides straightforward output indicating test status.

Key Takeaways for Writing Effective Unit Tests in Zig:

Write tests that are focused and test a specific unit of code (e.g., a function).

Choose descriptive names for your test cases.

Use assertions to clearly define the expected outcomes.

Test both success and failure scenarios, including error handling.

Organize your tests logically as your project grows.

Consider adopting a TDD workflow.

Zig's built-in testing framework is a valuable tool for building robust and reliable software. By embracing unit testing, you can catch bugs early in the development process and have more confidence in the correctness of your code.

7.2 Effective Debugging Techniques and Tools in Zig

You're asking about a crucial aspect of software development! Let's explore **Effective Debugging Techniques and Tools in Zig**. While Zig's focus on explicitness and safety can help reduce bugs, they are still inevitable. Here's a breakdown of how to effectively debug Zig code:

1. `std.debug.print` **for Basic Inspection:**

Just like in many other languages, the simplest debugging technique in Zig is using print statements to inspect the values of variables and the flow of execution. Zig provides `std.debug.print` for this purpose. Output from `std.debug.print` typically goes to the standard error stream.

Code snippet

```
const std = @import("std");

fn process(value: i32) i32 {
    std.debug.print("[DEBUG] Entering process with value: {}\n", .{value});
    const result = value * 2;
    std.debug.print("[DEBUG] Result before potential issue: {}\n", .{result});
    if (result > 10) {
        const adjusted = result - 5;
```

```zig
        std.debug.print("[DEBUG] Adjusted result: {}\n", .{adjusted});
        return adjusted;
    }
        std.debug.print("[DEBUG] Returning original result: {}\n",
.{result});
    return result;
}

pub fn main() !void {
    const input = 12;
    const output = process(input);
    std.debug.print("Output: {}\n", .{output});
}
```

Pros: Quick and easy for simple cases.

Cons: Can clutter code, requires manual insertion and removal, not ideal for complex state or stepping through execution.

2. Using a Debugger (LLDB with Zig):

For more in-depth debugging, using a proper debugger is essential. LLDB is the debugger commonly used with the Clang/LLVM toolchain, which Zig also utilizes.

Prerequisites:

Ensure you have LLDB installed on your system.

Compile your Zig code with debug information. You can do this by not specifying the -O flag for optimization (debug builds are the default) or by explicitly using -O 0.

Basic LLDB Workflow:

1.Compile with Debug Info:

2. Bash

```
zig build-exe your_program.zig
```
3.

4. This will create an executable (e.g., `your_program`).

5. **Start LLDB:**

6. Bash

```
lldb ./your_program
```
7.

8. This will start the LLDB session attached to your executable.

9. **Set Breakpoints:** Use the `breakpoint set` command to pause execution at specific locations (line numbers or function names).

10. Code snippet

```
breakpoint set --file your_program.zig --line 10  // Break at line 10
breakpoint set --name process                     // Break at the start of the 'process' function
```
11.

12. **Run the Program:** Use the `run` command to start the program execution within the debugger.

13. Code snippet

run
14.

15. **Stepping Through Code:**

`next` (or `n`): Execute the current line and move to the next line in the same function.

`step` (or `s`): Step into a function call on the current line.

`finish` (or `f`): Continue execution until the current function returns.

`continue` (or `c`): Continue execution until the next breakpoint is hit or the program exits.

16. **Inspecting Variables:** Use the `frame variable` (or `v`) command to print the values of local variables in the current stack frame.

17. Code snippet

frame variable value
frame variable result
18.

19. You can also inspect the contents of pointers and slices.

20. **Examining Memory:** Use the `memory read` (or `x`) command to examine raw memory.

21. Code snippet

memory read &value
memory read -c 20 &my_array[0] // Read 20 bytes starting at the address of the first element of my_array
22.

23. **Getting Stack Trace:** Use the `thread backtrace` (or `bt`) command to see the current call stack.

24. **Quitting LLDB:** Use the `quit` command to exit the debugger.

Pros: Powerful for stepping through code, inspecting complex state, examining memory, and understanding program flow.

Cons: Requires learning LLDB commands, can be more involved than simple printing.

3. Using a Graphical Debugger (e.g., VS Code with Zig Extension):

Integrated Development Environments (IDEs) like VS Code with the appropriate Zig extension can provide a more user-friendly debugging experience with a graphical interface.

Workflow (VS Code):

1.**Install Zig Extension:** Install the official or a well-regarded Zig extension in VS Code.

2. **Configure Launch Configuration:** Create a `launch.json` file in the `.vscode` directory of your project to configure how the debugger should be launched and attached to your Zig executable. A basic configuration might look like this:

3. JSON

```json
{
    "version": "0.2.0",
    "configurations": [
        {
            "name": "Debug Zig",
            "type": "lldb",
            "request": "launch",
            "program": "${workspaceFolder}/zig-out/bin/${workspaceFolderBasename}",
            "args": [],
            "cwd": "${workspaceFolder}",
            "terminal": "integrated",
```

```
        "preLaunchTask": "zig: build debug" // Assuming you have
a task to build in debug mode
    }
  ]
}
4.
```

5. **Set Breakpoints:** Click in the gutter next to the line numbers in your Zig code to set breakpoints.

6. **Start Debugging:** Go to the "Run and Debug" view in VS Code and start the "Debug Zig" configuration.

7. **Use Debug Controls:** Use the buttons at the top (Continue, Step Over, Step Into, Step Out, Restart, Disconnect) to control the execution.

8. **Inspect Variables:** The "Variables" pane will show the current values of local variables. You can also add variables to the "Watch" pane to monitor them.

9. **View Call Stack:** The "Call Stack" pane shows the sequence of function calls leading to the current execution point.

Pros: User-friendly graphical interface, integrated with the editor, often provides more features for inspecting variables and memory.

Cons: Requires setting up the IDE and extension, might have some Zig-specific limitations depending on the extension's maturity.

4. Leveraging Zig's Safety Features for Debugging:

Zig's design inherently helps with debugging:

Explicit Error Handling: The ! error union type forces you to handle potential errors, making it less likely for errors to propagate silently.

Optional Types (?T): Make the possibility of a null value explicit, reducing null pointer exceptions if handled correctly.

Bounds Checking (Debug Builds): Helps catch out-of-bounds array and slice accesses early.

No Implicit Control Flow: Makes it easier to follow the execution path.

5. Using `zig test` for Unit Testing and Debugging:

Well-written unit tests can be an invaluable debugging tool. When a bug arises, a failing test can pinpoint the exact location and conditions under which the bug occurs. You can also run specific tests in a debugger to examine the failing scenario.

6. Memory Sanitizers (Advanced):

For detecting memory-related errors like leaks, use-after-free, and out-of-bounds access, you can potentially integrate memory sanitizers like AddressSanitizer (ASan) or MemorySanitizer (MemSan) during compilation and testing (though direct integration might require some manual setup with the underlying LLVM tools).

7. Profiling (for Performance Issues):

While not strictly debugging for correctness, profiling tools can help identify performance bottlenecks in your Zig application, which might indirectly reveal logical issues or inefficient algorithms. You might be able to use standard system profiling tools (like `perf` on Linux or Instruments on macOS) with your Zig executables.

Effective Debugging Workflow:

1.**Understand the Problem:** Try to reproduce the bug and understand the conditions under which it occurs.

2. **Start Simple:** Use `std.debug.print` for initial investigation in straightforward cases.

3.**Isolate the Issue:** Try to narrow down the part of the code where the bug is likely happening.

4. **Use a Debugger:** For more complex issues, set breakpoints near the suspected area and step through the code.

5. **Inspect Variables and Memory:** Pay close attention to the values of variables and the state of memory as the program executes.

6. **Check the Call Stack:** Understand the sequence of function calls that led to the current point.

7. **Write Unit Tests:** Once you've found and fixed a bug, write a unit test to ensure it doesn't reappear.

8. **Be Systematic:** Follow a methodical approach to avoid getting lost in the debugging process.

By combining these techniques and tools, you can effectively diagnose and fix issues in your Zig programs. As the Zig ecosystem matures, we might see even more specialized debugging tools and integrations emerge.

7.3 Ensuring Code Quality and Reliability through Testing

You've hit on a cornerstone of good software development! **Ensuring Code Quality and Reliability through Testing** is not just a good practice; it's often a necessity for building robust and maintainable applications. Let's explore the various aspects of testing that contribute to code quality and reliability in the context of Zig and general software development.

Why is Testing Crucial for Code Quality and Reliability?

Bug Detection: Testing is the primary way to identify and expose defects (bugs) in your code before it reaches end-users. Early detection saves time, resources, and potential damage to reputation.

Verification of Requirements: Tests ensure that the software behaves as intended and meets the specified requirements. They act as executable specifications.

Regression Prevention: When you fix a bug, writing a test that specifically covers that bug ensures that the issue doesn't resurface in future changes.

Code Confidence: A comprehensive suite of tests gives developers more confidence when making changes or refactoring code, knowing that they have a safety net to catch unintended consequences.

Documentation through Examples: Tests often serve as living documentation, illustrating how different parts of the code are intended to be used.

Improved Design: Writing tests can often drive better code design by encouraging modularity, testability, and separation of concerns.

Types of Testing and Their Contribution:

1.Unit Testing (Focus on Small Units):

What it tests: Individual functions, methods, or small components of your code in isolation.

Contribution: Verifies the correctness of the fundamental building blocks of your application. Catches bugs at a granular level, making them easier to isolate and fix. Zig's built-in testing framework (`test` keyword) is ideal for unit testing.

2. Integration Testing (Focus on Interactions):

What it tests: How different units or components of your system interact with each other (e.g., modules within your application, interactions with databases, APIs).

Contribution: Ensures that the seams between different parts of your application work correctly together. Catches issues related to data flow, communication protocols, and shared state.

3. End-to-End (E2E) Testing (Focus on User Workflows):

What it tests: Complete user scenarios or workflows from the user's perspective, often involving multiple components and external systems.

Contribution: Validates that the entire system works as expected for the intended user experience. Catches high-level issues that might not be apparent in unit or integration tests.

4. Other Important Types of Testing:

Performance Testing: Evaluates the speed, responsiveness, and stability of the application under various load conditions.

Security Testing: Identifies vulnerabilities and ensures the application is protected against unauthorized access and attacks.

Usability Testing: Assesses how easy and intuitive the application is to use for end-users.

Accessibility Testing: Ensures that the application is usable by people with disabilities.

Strategies for Effective Testing:

Test Early and Often: Integrate testing throughout the development lifecycle, not just at the end.

Aim for High Test Coverage: Strive to test a significant portion of your codebase to increase confidence in its correctness. Coverage metrics can help identify areas that need more testing.

Write Independent and Repeatable Tests: Tests should not depend on external state or the order in which they are run. They should produce the same result every time.

Write Clear and Maintainable Tests: Tests should be easy to understand and maintain. Use descriptive names and avoid overly complex test logic.

Test Boundary Conditions and Edge Cases: Pay attention to inputs that are at the limits of what is expected or unusual scenarios that might reveal bugs.

Test Error Handling: Ensure that your application handles errors gracefully and as expected.

Mock External Dependencies: For unit and some integration tests, use mocks or stubs to isolate the unit under test from external systems that might be slow, unreliable, or difficult to set up.

Automate Your Tests: Integrate your tests into your build and continuous integration/continuous deployment (CI/CD) pipelines to ensure they are run automatically with every code change.

Testing in Zig:

As we discussed, Zig has a built-in testing framework for unit tests. For integration and E2E testing, you might need to build your own testing infrastructure or leverage external tools if needed. Zig's explicitness and low-level capabilities can be beneficial for writing tests that interact with system resources or have specific performance requirements.

The Role of Code Reviews:

While not strictly testing, code reviews are another crucial practice for ensuring code quality and reliability. Having other developers review your code can help catch logical errors, potential bugs, and areas for improvement that might be missed by automated tests.

In conclusion, ensuring code quality and reliability is a multifaceted effort that relies heavily on comprehensive testing at various levels. By adopting effective testing strategies and leveraging Zig's built-in testing framework, you can build more robust, maintainable, and dependable applications. Remember that testing is an ongoing process that should evolve alongside your codebase.

CHAPTER 8

Building Practical Applications: Networking Basics

8.1 Introduction to Network Programming Concepts (Sockets, Protocols)

Let's dive into the fundamental concepts of network programming: **Sockets** and **Protocols**. These are the building blocks that enable applications to communicate with each other across a network, whether it's a local network or the vast expanse of the internet.

1. Network Protocols: The Language of Communication

Imagine trying to have a conversation with someone who doesn't speak the same language or follow the same rules of communication. It would be chaotic and ineffective. Network protocols serve as the common language and set of rules that computers and network devices use to communicate effectively.

Definition: A network protocol is a standardized set of rules, procedures, and formats that govern how data is transmitted and received over a network. These rules ensure that devices, regardless of their hardware or software, can understand and interact with each other.

Key Aspects of Protocols:

Syntax: Defines the format and structure of the data being exchanged. Think of it as the grammar of the network language.

Semantics: Specifies the meaning of the data and the control information being transmitted. This is like the meaning of words in a language.

Timing: Dictates the order and speed of data transmission. This is akin to the pacing and flow of a conversation.

The OSI Model: To better understand the different layers of network communication and the protocols that operate at each layer, the Open Systems Interconnection (OSI) model is often used as a conceptual framework. It divides network communication into seven distinct layers, each with specific responsibilities and protocols.

Examples of Common Network Protocols:

HTTP/HTTPS (Hypertext Transfer Protocol/Secure): The foundation of the World Wide Web, used for transferring web pages and other content between web browsers and servers. HTTPS adds encryption for secure communication.

TCP (Transmission Control Protocol): A reliable, connection-oriented protocol that ensures ordered and error-checked delivery of data. It's used by many applications like web browsing, email, and file transfer.

IP (Internet Protocol): Responsible for addressing and routing data packets across networks. It works in conjunction with TCP (often referred to as TCP/IP).

UDP (User Datagram Protocol): A connectionless protocol that is faster but less reliable than TCP. It's often used for applications where speed is critical and occasional data loss is acceptable, such as streaming and online gaming.

DNS (Domain Name System): Translates human-readable domain names (like `google.com`) into IP addresses that computers use to locate each other.

SMTP (Simple Mail Transfer Protocol): Used for sending emails between mail servers.

FTP (File Transfer Protocol): Used for transferring files between a client and a server.

2. Sockets: The Endpoints of Communication

Now that we understand the language (protocols), we need to understand how applications actually send and receive this language over the network. This is where **sockets** come in.

Definition: A socket is a software construct that serves as an endpoint for sending and receiving data across a network. It's an abstraction layer that allows applications to interact with the network without needing to understand the low-level details of the underlying network protocols.

Analogy: Think of a socket as an electrical outlet. Different devices (applications) can plug into it to send and receive power (data). The type of plug and the way electricity flows are governed by electrical standards (protocols).

Socket Address: A socket is typically associated with a network address and a port number. This combination, known as a socket address, uniquely identifies a network process on a specific machine.

IP Address: Identifies the specific computer on the network.

Port Number: Identifies a specific application or service running on that computer. Port numbers allow multiple network applications to run on the same machine simultaneously.

Types of Sockets:

TCP Sockets (Stream Sockets): Provide a reliable, ordered, and connection-oriented communication channel. Data is treated as a continuous stream of bytes. Before data can be exchanged, a connection must be established between the client and the server (using a process called a three-way handshake).

UDP Sockets (Datagram Sockets): Provide a connectionless and unreliable communication channel. Data is sent in independent packets called datagrams. There's no guarantee of delivery or the order in which packets arrive. This makes UDP faster but less suitable for applications requiring guaranteed delivery.

The Client-Server Model: Network programming often follows the client-server model:

Server: An application that listens for incoming connection requests on a specific socket (IP address and port). When a client connects, the server typically creates a new socket to handle the communication with that specific client.

Client: An application that initiates a connection to a server's socket. Once the connection is established (for TCP) or it knows the server's address and port (for UDP), the client can send and receive data.

In Summary:

Network protocols are the rules and language that govern network communication, ensuring that different systems can understand each other.

Sockets are the programming interface that allows applications to send and receive data over a network using specific protocols. They act as endpoints for network communication and are identified by an IP address and a port number.

Understanding these fundamental concepts is the first step towards building network applications in any programming language, including Zig. You'll use socket APIs provided by the standard library or external libraries to create, bind, listen, connect, send, and receive data over a network, adhering to specific network protocols to ensure successful communication.

8.2 Implementing Basic Network Communication in Zig (TCP/UDP)

Alright, let's get our hands dirty and look at how to implement basic network communication in Zig using TCP and UDP. Zig's standard library provides the `std.net` module for this purpose.

1. TCP Communication:

TCP is connection-oriented, reliable, and ensures ordered delivery of data. It's commonly used for applications like web servers, email clients, and file transfer.

TCP Server:

Code snippet

```
const std = @import("std");
const net = std.net;
const os = std.os;

const PORT: u16 = 8080;

pub fn main() !void {
    const listener = try net.tcp.listen(net.Address.ipv4(net.Ipv4{
.address = .{ 0, 0, 0, 0 }, .port = PORT }));
    defer listener.close();
    std.debug.print("TCP Server listening on port {}\n", .{PORT});

    while (true) {
        const connection = try listener.accept();
        os.spawn(.{}, handleConnection, .{ .connection = connection
}) catch |err| {
            std.debug.print("Error spawning connection handler: {}\n",
.{err});
            connection.close();
        };
    }
}

fn handleConnection(args: struct { connection: net.tcp.Connection
}) !void {
    defer args.connection.close();
    const connection = args.connection;
    var buf: [1024]u8 = undefined;
```

```
while (true) {
    const result = connection.read(&buf);
    if (result == 0) {
        std.debug.print("Client disconnected.\n", .{});
        break;
    } else if (result < 0) {
            std.debug.print("Error reading from connection: {}\n",
.{result});
        break;
    } else {
        const bytes_read = @as(usize, result);
            std.debug.print("Received {} bytes: {}\n", .{bytes_read,
buf[0..bytes_read]});

        // Echo back the received data
        try connection.writeAll(buf[0..bytes_read]);
    }
  }
}
```

To run the TCP server:

1.Save the code as `tcp_server.zig`.

2. Compile and run: `zig run tcp_server.zig`

TCP Client:

Code snippet

```
const std = @import("std");
const net = std.net;
const os = std.os;
```

```zig
const SERVER_ADDRESS = "127.0.0.1";
const SERVER_PORT: u16 = 8080;

pub fn main() !void {
    const address = try net.Address.parseIp(SERVER_ADDRESS,
SERVER_PORT);
    const connection = try net.tcp.connect(address);
    defer connection.close();
    std.debug.print("Connected to {}:{}\n", .{SERVER_ADDRESS,
SERVER_PORT});

    const message = "Hello from Zig TCP Client!";
    try connection.writeAll(message);
    std.debug.print("Sent: {}\n", .{message});

    var buf: [1024]u8 = undefined;
    const bytes_read = try connection.read(&buf);
    std.debug.print("Received {} bytes: {}\n", .{bytes_read});
    if (bytes_read > 0) {
                        std.debug.print("Echo   from   server:   {}\n",
.{buf[0..bytes_read]});
    }
}
```

To run the TCP client:

1.Save the code as `tcp_client.zig`.

2. Compile and run (after starting the server): `zig run tcp_client.zig`

Explanation:

TCP Server:

`net.tcp.listen`: Creates a TCP listener socket bound to the specified address and port.

`listener.accept`: Blocks until a client tries to connect and returns a `net.tcp.Connection` object representing the connection.

`os.spawn`: Creates a new lightweight thread to handle each incoming connection concurrently.

`connection.read`: Reads data from the client. Returns the number of bytes read (0 if the client disconnected, negative on error).

`connection.writeAll`: Sends data back to the client.

`connection.close`: Closes the connection.

The server runs in an infinite loop, accepting new connections.

TCP Client:

`net.Address.parseIp`: Parses the server address and port.

`net.tcp.connect`: Establishes a TCP connection to the server.

`connection.writeAll`: Sends data to the server.

`connection.read`: Reads the server's response.

`connection.close`: Closes the connection.

2. UDP Communication:

UDP is connectionless and unreliable but often faster. It's suitable for applications like DNS, streaming, and some online games.

UDP Server:

Code snippet

```
const std = @import("std");
const net = std.net;

const PORT: u16 = 8081;
const MAX_PACKET_SIZE: usize = 1024;

pub fn main() !void {
    const socket = try net.udp.bind(net.Address.ipv4(net.Ipv4{
.address = .{ 0, 0, 0, 0 }, .port = PORT }));
    defer socket.close();
    std.debug.print("UDP Server listening on port {}\n", .{PORT});

    var buf: [MAX_PACKET_SIZE]u8 = undefined;
    var peer_address: net.Address = undefined;

    while (true) {
        const bytes_received = try socket.recv(&buf, &peer_address);
```

```
            std.debug.print("Received {} bytes from {}: {}\n",
.{bytes_received, peer_address, buf[0..bytes_received]});

    // Echo back to the sender
    try socket.send(peer_address, buf[0..bytes_received]);
  }
}
```

To run the UDP server:

1.Save the code as `udp_server.zig`.

2. Compile and run: `zig run udp_server.zig`

UDP Client:

Code snippet

```
const std = @import("std");
const net = std.net;

const SERVER_ADDRESS = "127.0.0.1";
const SERVER_PORT: u16 = 8081;

pub fn main() !void {
    const server_address = try net.Address.parseIp(SERVER_ADDRESS, SERVER_PORT);
    const socket = try net.udp.open(.{});
    defer socket.close();

    const message = "Hello from Zig UDP Client!";
    try socket.send(server_address, message);
    std.debug.print("Sent: {}\n", .{message});

    var buf: [1024]u8 = undefined;
```

```
    var peer_address: net.Address = undefined;
    const bytes_received = try socket.recv(&buf, &peer_address);
        std.debug.print("Received  {}  bytes  from  {}:  {}\n",
.{bytes_received, peer_address, buf[0..bytes_received]});
    if (bytes_received > 0) {
                    std.debug.print("Echo  from  server:  {}\n",
.{buf[0..bytes_received]});
    }
}
```

To run the UDP client:

1.Save the code as `udp_client.zig`.

2. Compile and run (after starting the server): `zig run udp_client.zig`

Explanation:

UDP Server:

`net.udp.bind`: Creates a UDP socket bound to the specified address and port.

`socket.recv`: Receives a UDP packet into the buffer and also gets the address of the sender (`peer_address`).

`socket.send`: Sends a UDP packet to the specified address.

The server runs in an infinite loop, receiving and echoing back packets.

UDP Client:

`net.Address.parseIp`: Parses the server address and port.

`net.udp.open`: Creates a UDP socket (it doesn't need to "connect" in the TCP sense).

`socket.send`: Sends a UDP packet to the server's address.

`socket.recv`: Waits for a response from the server and gets the sender's address.

Important Considerations:

Error Handling: The examples use `try` to propagate errors. In real-world applications, you'd want more robust error handling.

Concurrency (TCP Server): The TCP server uses `os.spawn` to handle multiple connections concurrently. For more complex applications, you might want to explore Zig's `async/await` for managing concurrency, especially for I/O-bound tasks.

Packet Size (UDP): UDP has limitations on packet size. Exceeding these limits can lead to fragmentation and potential loss.

Addressing: The examples use IPv4 addresses (`net.Ipv4`). Zig also supports IPv6 (`net.Ipv6`).

Byte Order: When sending binary data across networks, be mindful of byte order (endianness) and use functions like `std.net.toNetworkOrder` and `std.net.fromNetworkOrder` if necessary.

These examples provide a basic foundation for implementing TCP and UDP network communication in Zig. You can build upon these concepts to create more sophisticated network applications.

8.3 Handling Network Errors and Building Robust Networked Applications

Building robust networked applications requires careful consideration of potential network errors and implementing strategies to handle them gracefully. Networks are inherently unreliable, and many things can go wrong during communication. Here's a breakdown of common network errors and techniques for building robust networked applications in Zig:

1. Common Network Errors:

Connection Errors (TCP):

Connection Refused: The server actively refused the connection attempt.

Connection Timed Out: No response was received from the server within a certain time.

Host Unreachable: The destination host could not be found.

Network Unreachable: The network path to the destination is unavailable.

Connection Reset: The connection was forcibly closed by the peer.

Read/Write Errors (TCP & UDP):

Connection Reset by Peer: The other end closed the connection during data transfer.

Broken Pipe: Attempting to write to a connection that has been closed by the peer.

Timeout: A read or write operation took longer than the configured timeout.

Resource Unavailable: The system might be temporarily unable to allocate resources for the operation.

UDP Specific Errors:

Packet Loss: UDP packets can be lost in transit without notification.

Packet Corruption: Packets can be corrupted during transmission.

Out-of-Order Delivery: UDP packets might arrive in a different order than they were sent.

DNS Errors:

Host Not Found: Unable to resolve a domain name to an IP address.

Timeout: DNS resolution took too long.

Other Errors:

Invalid Arguments: Providing incorrect parameters to network functions.

Address Already in Use: Trying to bind a socket to an address and port that is already in use.

Permission Denied: The application doesn't have the necessary permissions for a network operation.

2. Techniques for Handling Network Errors in Zig:

Check Error Returns: Zig's network functions in `std.net` typically return `Result` types (using `!Error`) or error codes. Always check the return value to see if an error occurred. Use `if (err) |e| { ... }` or `try` with `catch` to handle errors.

Code snippet

```
const std = @import("std");
const net = std.net;
```

```
pub fn connectToServer(address: net.Address) !net.tcp.Connection
{
    const connection = net.tcp.connect(address) catch |err| {
        std.debug.print("Error connecting: {}\n", .{err});
        return err;
    };
    return connection;
}
```

Retry Mechanisms: For transient errors like connection timeouts or temporary network issues, implementing a retry mechanism with exponential backoff can improve robustness. Be careful to limit the number of retries to avoid overwhelming the network or server.

Code snippet

```
const std = @import("std");
const net = std.net;
const time = std.time;

pub fn connectWithRetry(address: net.Address, max_retries: u32)
!net.tcp.Connection {
    for (0..max_retries) |i| {
        const connection_result = net.tcp.connect(address);
        if (connection_result) |conn| {
            return conn;
        } else |err| {
            std.debug.print("Attempt {} failed: {}\n", .{i + 1, err});
```

```
    if (i < max_retries - 1) {
            await time.sleep(time.milliseconds(@as(u64, 100 << i)));
// Exponential backoff
        }
      }
    }
    return error.ConnectionFailed;
}
```

Timeouts: Set appropriate timeouts for connection establishment, read, and write operations to prevent your application from hanging indefinitely due to network issues. Zig's `std.net.Socket` and connection types often have options for setting timeouts.

Code snippet

```
const std = @import("std");
const net = std.net;
const time = std.time;

pub fn readWithTimeout(connection: *net.tcp.Connection, buf: []u8,
timeout: time.Duration) !usize {
    connection.setReadTimeout(timeout);
    const result = connection.read(buf);
        connection.setReadTimeout(std.math.maxInt(u64));  // Reset
timeout
    return result;
}
```

Connection Management (TCP): Implement proper connection management, including closing connections when they are no longer needed and handling graceful shutdowns. Be prepared for unexpected connection closures from the peer.

Idempotent Operations: Design your network interactions to be idempotent where possible. An idempotent operation can be repeated multiple times with the same effect as performing it once. This helps in handling retries safely.

Logging and Monitoring: Implement comprehensive logging to record network events, errors, and performance metrics. This helps in diagnosing issues and understanding the behavior of your application in production. Consider using monitoring tools to track the health and performance of your networked application.

Graceful Degradation: Design your application to handle network failures gracefully. For example, if a connection to a non-critical service fails, the application might continue to function with reduced functionality instead of crashing.

Keep-Alive Mechanisms (TCP): For long-lived TCP connections, consider using keep-alive probes to detect and handle dead connections.

Error Codes and Messages: When communicating with other applications, establish clear error codes and messages to provide more context about failures.

Testing Network Faults: During development and testing, try to simulate various network error conditions (e.g., network outages, server not responding, packet loss) to ensure your application handles them correctly. Tools for network simulation can be helpful.

Asynchronous Operations: Using asynchronous programming (`async`/`await` in Zig) can help prevent your main application thread from blocking while waiting for network operations, improving responsiveness even during network latency or failures.

UDP Considerations: For UDP, since it's unreliable, you might need to implement your own mechanisms for reliability if required, such as acknowledgements, sequence numbers, and retransmissions. Be mindful of the added complexity and potential performance impact.

Building Robust Networked Applications in Zig:

Embrace Error Handling: Treat network errors as a normal part of operation and handle them explicitly.

Design for Resilience: Build your application with the expectation that network connections can be flaky and temporary failures can occur.

Provide Informative Feedback: Log errors and provide meaningful feedback to users or administrators when network issues arise.

Thorough Testing: Rigorously test your application's behavior under various network conditions.

By implementing these techniques and being mindful of the inherent challenges of network communication, you can build more robust and reliable networked applications in Zig. Remember that the specific error handling strategies you employ will depend on the requirements and criticality of your application.

CHAPTER 9

Building Practical Applications: File System Interaction

9.1 Working with Files and Directories in Zig (Reading, Writing, Manipulation)

Okay, let's think about working with files and folders in Zig using a different analogy – imagine your computer's storage as a big filing cabinet.

Files: The Documents Inside

Think of files as individual documents stored in this filing cabinet. To work with a document, you first need to:

1.**Open the Drawer (Open the File):** Before you can read or write on a document, you need to open the correct drawer in the filing cabinet. In Zig, this is like using `std.fs.openFile`. You tell Zig which document (file path) you want and what you want to do with it (read, write, or both).

Reading: It's like opening a document to read what's written on it.

Writing: It's like opening a blank document or an existing one to add or change the text. You might even decide to create a new document if it doesn't exist.

2. **Read the Document (Read from File):** Once the drawer is open and you have the document, you can read its contents.

Reading bit by bit (Reading into a buffer): Imagine reading a document sentence by sentence, copying each sentence onto a separate piece of paper you have (your buffer). `file.read` in Zig does something similar – it reads a chunk of the file's content into a temporary storage area you provide.

Reading the whole document at once (Reading the entire file into a dynamically allocated buffer): Sometimes, you just want to photocopy the entire document. `fs.readFileAlloc` is like that – it makes a copy of the whole file's content and gives it to you. Just remember, like a photocopy, you'll need to get rid of it when you're done (free the memory).

Reading line by line (Reading with a buffered reader): If the document is organized into lines, you might want to read it one line at a time. `std.io.bufferedReader` helps you do this, letting you grab each line sequentially.

3. **Write on the Document (Write to File):** If you opened the document for writing, you can add or modify its contents.

Writing a small note (Writing a buffer): You might just want to jot down a quick note on the document. `file.write` lets you write a small piece of data (your note) into the file.

Writing everything you have (Writing all data from a buffer): If you have a whole page of text you want to add, `file.writeAll` ensures that everything you have gets written to the document.

Writing in a specific format (Writing formatted output): Sometimes, you want to write information in a structured way, like adding a date and a log message. `std.fmt.format` helps you prepare this structured text before you write it to the file.

4. **Close the Drawer (Close the File):** When you're finished with a document, it's important to put it back in the drawer and close the drawer. This is like `file.close()` in Zig – it tells the system you're done with the file, so other programs can access it and system resources are freed up.

Directories/Folders: The Filing Cabinet Drawers

Now, think of directories or folders as the drawers in our filing cabinet. They help organize our documents (files).

1. **Creating a New Drawer (Creating a directory):** If you need to organize your documents better, you might add a new drawer. `fs.makeDir` in Zig creates a new, empty folder. If you need to create a series of nested drawers all at once (like a drawer inside a drawer), you'd use `fs.makeDirRecursive`.

2. **Removing a Drawer (Deleting a directory):** If a drawer is empty and no longer needed, you can remove it with `fs.rmDir`. If the drawer has documents or other drawers inside it, you'd need to use `fs.rmDirRecursive` (but be very careful, this is like emptying and then throwing away the entire drawer and everything in it!).

3. **Looking Inside a Drawer (Listing directory contents):** To see what documents (files) are in a drawer, you open it and look at the labels. `fs.Dir.open` opens a directory, and then you can use a

loop with `dir.next()` to see the name and type of each item inside (whether it's a file or another drawer).

4.**Checking if a Drawer or Document Exists (Checking if a path exists and its type):** Before you try to open a specific document or drawer, you might want to check if it's actually there. `fs.exists` tells you if something at a given path exists, and `fs.stat` gives you more information, like whether it's a file or a directory.

5. **Changing the Label on a Drawer or Document (Renaming):** If you want to change the name of a document or a drawer, you'd change its label. `fs.rename` in Zig lets you rename files and directories.

6. **Getting Rid of a Document (Deleting a file):** If you no longer need a specific document, you can throw it away (delete the file) using `fs.deleteFile`.

Key Things to Remember:

Always open before using: Just like you need to open a drawer or a document, you need to open files and directories in Zig before you can work with them.

Always close when done: Just like closing a drawer keeps things organized, closing files with `defer file.close()` releases resources.

Be careful with deletion: Removing drawers and documents permanently gets rid of them, so use `fs.rmDirRecursive` and `fs.deleteFile` with caution.

Expect things to go wrong: Just like a drawer might be locked or a document might be missing, file and directory operations can fail (e.g., file not found, no permission). Always handle potential errors using `try` and `catch`.

This analogy of a filing cabinet should give you a different way to understand the basic concepts of working with files and directories in Zig. The Zig code then provides the specific instructions on how to interact with this "filing cabinet" using the `std.fs` module.

9.2 Handling File System Errors and Permissions

You're highlighting a critical aspect of working with files and directories! Just like in the real world, interacting with the file system can encounter various issues. Handling these errors gracefully and understanding permissions are essential for building reliable applications. Let's break down common file system errors and how to address them in Zig.

1. Common File System Errors:

File Not Found: Attempting to open, read, or delete a file that doesn't exist.

Directory Not Found: Trying to operate on a directory that doesn't exist.

Permission Denied: The application lacks the necessary permissions to perform the requested operation (e.g., reading a protected file, writing to a restricted directory, creating a file in a read-only location).

Path Not Found: A component in the specified path (other than the final file or directory name) does not exist.

Is a Directory: Attempting to perform a file operation on a directory (e.g., trying to read from a directory).

Not a Directory: Attempting to perform a directory operation on a file (e.g., trying to list the contents of a file).

Disk Full: No more space available on the storage device.

Device Not Available: The storage device is not accessible.

File Already Exists: Trying to create a file with a name that already exists when the operation doesn't allow overwriting.

Invalid Filename: The provided filename contains characters that are not allowed by the operating system's file system.

Too Many Open Files: The application has exceeded the system's limit on the number of open file handles.

2. Handling File System Errors in Zig:

Zig's strong error handling机制, using the ! syntax for error unions and the `try/catch` mechanism, is crucial for dealing with file system operations.

Checking Error Returns: Most functions in `std.fs` that can fail return an error union. Always check the result of these functions.

Code snippet

```
const std = @import("std");
const fs = std.fs;
```

```
pub fn readFileSafely(path: []const u8) !?[]const u8 {
    const file = try fs.openFile(path, .{}, 0) catch |err| {
        std.debug.print("Error opening file '{}': {}\n", .{path, err});
        return null; // Or a more specific error
    };
    defer file.close();
        return try fs.readFileAlloc(std.heap.page_allocator, file,
std.math.maxInt(usize));
}

pub fn main() !void {
    const contents = try readFileSafely("my_file.txt");
    if (contents) |c| {
        defer std.heap.page_allocator.free(c);
        std.debug.print("File contents: {}\n", .{c});
    } else {
        std.debug.print("Failed to read file.\n", .{});
    }
}
```

Using `try` **and** `catch`**:** Employ `try` to execute file system operations and `catch` to handle specific error types. You can switch on the error to handle different scenarios.

Code snippet

```
const std = @import("std");
const fs = std.fs;
const os = std.os;
```

```
pub fn createFile(path: []const u8) !void {
    try fs.openFile(path, .{}, os.O_WRONLY | os.O_CREAT |
os.O_EXCL) catch |err| {
        if (err == error.FileExists) {
            std.debug.print("File '{}' already exists.\n", .{path});
            return;
        } else if (err == error.PermissionDenied) {
                std.debug.print("Permission denied to create '{}'.\n",
.{path});
            return err;
        } else {
            std.debug.print("Error creating file '{}': {}\n", .{path, err});
            return err;
        }
    };
    std.debug.print("File '{}' created successfully.\n", .{path});
}

pub fn main() !void {
    try createFile("new_file.txt");
}
```

Checking File Existence: Before attempting to operate on a file or directory, you can use `fs.exists` to check if it exists.

Code snippet

```
const std = @import("std");
const fs = std.fs;
```

```
pub fn deleteFileIfExists(path: []const u8) !void {
    if (try fs.exists(path)) {
        try fs.deleteFile(path);
        std.debug.print("Deleted file '{}'.\n", .{path});
    } else {
        std.debug.print("File '{}' does not exist, nothing to delete.\n",
.{path});
    }
}

pub fn main() !void {
    try deleteFileIfExists("maybe_exists.txt");
}
```

3. Understanding File System Permissions:

File system permissions control who can access and modify files and directories. The way permissions are represented varies between operating systems (e.g., POSIX-based systems like Linux and macOS use a system of owners, groups, and others with read, write, and execute permissions; Windows uses Access Control Lists (ACLs)).

Zig's Abstraction: Zig's standard library provides some abstraction over permissions, but for fine-grained control, you might need to use OS-specific APIs. The mode argument in functions like fs.makeDir often uses POSIX-style octal representations (e.g., 0o755).

Code snippet

```zig
const std = @import("std");
const fs = std.fs;

pub fn createRestrictedDirectory(path: []const u8) !void {
    // 0o700: Owner has read, write, execute; group and others
    have no permissions
    try fs.makeDir(path, 0o700);
    std.debug.print("Created restricted directory '{}'.\n", .{path});
}

pub fn main() !void {
    try createRestrictedDirectory("restricted_dir");
}
```

Checking Permissions (More OS-Specific): Directly querying detailed permissions might require using OS-specific system calls. Zig's `std.os` module provides access to these. For example, on POSIX systems, you might use `os.chmod`, `os.stat`, and related functions (though these are lower-level).

Code snippet

```zig
const std = @import("std");
const fs = std.fs;
const os = std.os;

// This is a simplified example and might need more robust
handling
fn isWritable(path: []const u8) !bool {
```

```
    const stat = try fs.stat(path);
    // This checks the owner's write permission on POSIX-like
systems
    return (stat.mode & os.S_IWUSR) != 0;
}

pub fn main() !void {
    const file_path = "test_file.txt";
    if (try fs.exists(file_path)) {
        const writable = try isWritable(file_path);
        std.debug.print("{} is writable: {}\n", .{file_path, writable});
    } else {
        std.debug.print("{} does not exist.\n", .{file_path});
    }
}
```

Best Practices for Handling File System Errors and Permissions:

Anticipate Errors: Think about the potential errors that can occur for each file system operation you perform.

Handle Errors Gracefully: Don't just crash your application. Provide informative error messages to the user or log the errors for debugging.

Check Permissions Before Operations: If possible, check if your application has the necessary permissions before attempting a potentially failing operation.

Use Specific Error Handling: Catch specific error types to provide tailored responses (e.g., inform the user if a file doesn't exist versus a permission issue).

Consider Platform Differences: Be aware that file system behavior and permissions can vary significantly between operating systems. If your application needs to be cross-platform, you might need to handle these differences.

Minimize Privilege: Run your application with the minimum necessary privileges to reduce the risk of security vulnerabilities.

Inform Users About Permissions: If your application requires specific file system permissions, clearly communicate this to the user during installation or setup.

By diligently handling file system errors and being mindful of permissions, you can create more robust and user-friendly applications in Zig that interact reliably with the file system. Remember to consult the Zig standard library documentation for the most up-to-date and detailed information on file system operations and error types.

9.3 Building Utilities for File Processing and Management

Alright, let's talk about building **Utilities for File Processing and Management** in Zig. Zig's low-level capabilities, combined with its standard library, make it well-suited for creating efficient and reliable command-line tools or libraries for handling files and directories.

Here's a breakdown of common tasks and how you might approach building such utilities in Zig:

1. Core Functionality:

Reading File Contents:

For small to medium-sized files, `std.fs.readFileAlloc` is convenient to read the entire content into memory.

For larger files, use buffered reading (`std.io.bufferedReader` with `readLineAlloc` or manual buffer management with `file.read`) to process data in chunks, avoiding excessive memory usage.

Writing to Files:

`file.writeAll` is straightforward for writing a complete buffer to a file.

For more complex writing scenarios (e.g., formatting), use `std.fmt.format` to create the string and then write it.

For appending to files, use the appropriate open mode (`os.O_APPEND`).

File Copying:

Implement a function that opens the source file for reading and the destination file for writing, then reads data in chunks from the source and writes it to the destination until the entire file is copied. Handle potential errors during reading and writing.

File Deletion:

Use `std.fs.deleteFile` to remove a file. Handle the case where the file doesn't exist or permissions prevent deletion.

File Renaming/Moving:

`std.fs.rename` can be used to rename a file within the same file system or move it to a different directory on the same file system.

Directory Creation:

`std.fs.makeDir` creates a new directory.

`std.fs.makeDirRecursive` creates parent directories if they don't exist.

Directory Listing:

Open a directory with `std.fs.Dir.open` and iterate through its entries using `dir.next()`. You can then access the entry's name and kind (file, directory, etc.).

Directory Deletion (Recursive):

Implement a recursive function that iterates through the contents of a directory. For each entry, if it's a file, delete it. If it's a subdirectory, recursively call the deletion function on it, and then finally delete the empty subdirectory itself. Be extremely cautious with recursive deletion.

File Information (Metadata):

`std.fs.stat` retrieves information about a file or directory (size, modification time, permissions, etc.).

2. Building Command-Line Utilities:

Argument Parsing: Use `std.process.args()` to access command-line arguments. You might want to use a library (or build your own) for more sophisticated argument parsing (e.g., handling options, flags).

Standard Input/Output: Use `std.io.getStdIn().reader()` to read from standard input and `std.io.getStdOut().writer()` or `std.debug.print` to write to standard output/error.

Error Handling: Implement robust error handling for file system operations and provide informative error messages to the user on the command line. Use non-zero exit codes to indicate failure.

User Feedback: Provide feedback to the user about the progress of operations, especially for long-running tasks.

3. Examples of Utility Functions:

Code snippet

```
const std = @import("std");
```

```zig
const fs = std.fs;
const io = std.io;
const os = std.os;

// Reads the entire content of a file into a string
pub fn readFileString(allocator: std.mem.Allocator, path: []const u8) !?[]const u8 {
        const contents = try fs.readFileAlloc(allocator, path, std.math.maxInt(usize)) catch |err| {
        std.debug.print("Error reading file '{}': {}\n", .{path, err});
        return null;
    };
    return contents;
}


// Writes a string to a file
pub fn writeFileString(path: []const u8, contents: []const u8) !void {
        const file = try fs.openFile(path, .{}, os.O_WRONLY | os.O_CREAT | os.O_TRUNC) catch |err| {
        std.debug.print("Error opening file '{}' for writing: {}\n", .{path, err});
        return err;
    };
    defer file.close();
    try file.writeAll(contents);
}

// Copies a file from source to destination
pub fn copyFile(src: []const u8, dest: []const u8) !void {
   const src_file = try fs.openFile(src, .{}, 0) catch |err| {
        std.debug.print("Error opening source file '{}': {}\n", .{src, err});
        return err;
    };
    defer src_file.close();
```

```
    const dest_file = try fs.openFile(dest, .{}, os.O_WRONLY |
os.O_CREAT | os.O_TRUNC) catch |err| {
        std.debug.print("Error opening destination file '{}': {}\n", .{dest,
err});
        return err;
    };
    defer dest_file.close();

    var buffer: [4096]u8 = undefined;
    while (true) {
        const bytes_read = try src_file.read(&buffer);
        if (bytes_read == 0) break;
        try dest_file.writeAll(buffer[0..bytes_read]);
    }
}

// Recursively deletes a directory and its contents (USE WITH
EXTREME CAUTION)
pub fn deleteDirectoryRecursive(path: []const u8) !void {
    const dir = try fs.Dir.open(path, .{});
    defer dir.close();

    while (try dir.next()) |entry| {
        const full_path = try std.fs.path.join(std.heap.page_allocator,
&.{ path, entry.name });
        defer std.heap.page_allocator.free(full_path);

        if (entry.kind == .File) {
            try fs.deleteFile(full_path);
            std.debug.print("Deleted file: {}\n", .{full_path});
        } else if (entry.kind == .Directory) {
            try deleteDirectoryRecursive(full_path);
        }
    }
    try fs.rmDir(path);
```

```zig
        std.debug.print("Deleted directory: {}\n", .{path});
}

pub fn main() !void {
    const allocator = std.heap.page_allocator;

    // Example usage:
    if (readFileString(allocator, "input.txt")) |contents| {
        defer allocator.free(contents);
        std.debug.print("Contents of input.txt: {}\n", .{contents});
        try writeFileString("output.txt", contents);
        std.debug.print("Wrote contents to output.txt\n", .{});
    } else {
        std.debug.print("Failed to read input.txt\n", .{});
    }

    try copyFile("input.txt", "backup.txt");
    std.debug.print("Copied input.txt to backup.txt\n", .{});

        // Create and then recursively delete a directory (for
demonstration - be careful!)
    const test_dir = "test_dir";
     try fs.makeDirRecursive(try std.fs.path.join(allocator, &.{test_dir,
"subdir"}), 0o755);
        try writeFileString(try std.fs.path.join(allocator, &.{test_dir,
"file.txt"}), "test content");
    try deleteDirectoryRecursive(test_dir);
    std.debug.print("Deleted test directory recursively\n", .{});
}
```

4. Libraries and Frameworks:

As the Zig ecosystem grows, you might find or build libraries that provide higher-level abstractions for common file processing and management tasks, such as:

Handling different file formats (e.g., CSV, JSON, YAML).

More advanced argument parsing.

Progress bars for long operations.

More robust cross-platform path manipulation.

Key Considerations:

Error Handling: File system operations are prone to errors. Implement comprehensive error handling to make your utilities robust.

Resource Management: Always close files and free allocated memory to prevent leaks. Use `defer`.

Performance: For large files or frequent operations, consider buffering and efficient algorithms.

User Experience: For command-line utilities, provide clear and helpful output to the user.

Security: Be mindful of potential security risks when handling file paths and user input. Avoid vulnerabilities like path traversal.

Cross-Platform Compatibility: Test your utilities on different operating systems to ensure they work as expected. Use `std.fs.path` for platform-independent path manipulation where possible.

Building effective file processing and management utilities in Zig involves understanding the underlying file system APIs and applying good programming practices, especially around error handling and resource management. As you build more complex tools, consider modularizing your code and potentially creating reusable libraries.

CHAPTER 10

Advanced Zig and Real-World Deployments

10.1 Metaprogramming and Code Generation with Zig

Alright, let's delve into the fascinating world of **Metaprogramming and Code Generation with Zig**. Zig offers powerful features that allow you to write code that manipulates other code at compile time. This can lead to more efficient, flexible, and maintainable programs by automating repetitive tasks and generating specialized code based on compile-time information.

What is Metaprogramming?

Metaprogramming is the ability of a program to treat other programs as their data. This means you can write code that can inspect, modify, or generate other code. In Zig, this is primarily achieved through features that operate during the compilation process.

Key Metaprogramming Features in Zig:

1.**Compile-Time Functions** (`comptime`):

Functions marked with the `comptime` keyword are executed at compile time.

They can perform computations, make decisions based on compile-time constants, and return values that influence the generated code.

`comptime` functions are essential for many metaprogramming tasks.

2.Code snippet

```
const std = @import("std");

comptime fn powerOfTwo(n: u32) u32 {
    return if (n == 0) 1 else powerOfTwo(n - 1) * 2;
}

pub fn main() !void {
    const four = powerOfTwo(2); // Computed at compile time
    std.debug.print("2 to the power of 2 is {}\n", .{four});

    const sixteen: u32 = powerOfTwo(4); // Also compile-time
    std.debug.print("2 to the power of 4 is {}\n", .{sixteen});
}
```
3.

4. Compile-Time Variables and Constants:

`const` variables whose values are known at compile time can be used within `comptime` functions and to influence code generation.

5. Code snippet

```
const ARRAY_SIZE: comptime usize = 5;
var myArray: [ARRAY_SIZE]i32 = undefined;
```
6.

7. @Type **and Type Introspection:**

Zig allows you to work with types as first-class values using @Type.

You can inspect the properties of types at compile time (e.g., size, alignment, fields of a struct).

8.Code snippet

```
const std = @import("std");

comptime fn printTypeInfo(T: type) void {
    std.debug.print("Type: {}\n", .{@typeName(T)});
    std.debug.print("Size: {}\n", .{@sizeOf(T)});
    std.debug.print("Alignment: {}\n", .{@alignOf(T)});
}

pub fn main() !void {
    printTypeInfo(i32);
    printTypeInfo(f64);
    printTypeInfo(struct { x: i32, y: bool });
}
```
9.

10. **Compile-Time Blocks (**`comptime { ... }`**):**

Code within a `comptime` block is executed at compile time. It can perform setup or generate data that is then used in the rest of the program.

11. Code snippet

```
const std = @import("std");

comptime {
        std.debug.print("[COMETIME] This executes during compilation.\n", .{});
   // You could perform file I/O or other compile-time setup here.
}

pub fn main() !void {
   std.debug.print("[RUNTIME] This executes at runtime.\n", .{});
}
12.
```

13. **Code Generation with String Literals and** `@embedFile`**:**

While not full-fledged code generation in the sense of building ASTs, you can use string literals and `@embedFile` within `comptime` contexts to include external data or generate textual code that might be used in your program (though this is often less structured than other approaches).

14. **Zig Build System Integration:**

The Zig build system (`build.zig`) itself is written in Zig and executed at compile time. This allows for powerful metaprogramming to configure the build process, generate source files, and perform other build-time tasks.

Code Generation Patterns:

Generic Code Specialization: Generate specialized versions of functions or data structures based on compile-time type parameters or constants. This can improve performance by avoiding runtime branching or type conversions.

Code snippet

```
const std = @import("std");

comptime fn createArray(comptime T: type, size: comptime usize,
initial_value: T) []T {
    var result = [_]T{initial_value} ** size;
    return &result;
}

pub fn main() !void {
    const intArray = createArray(i32, 3, 10);
    std.debug.print("Int Array: {}\n", .{intArray}); // [10, 10, 10]

    const boolArray = createArray(bool, 2, true);
```

```
    std.debug.print("Bool Array: {}\n", .{boolArray}); // [true, true]
}
```

Automated Boilerplate Generation: Generate repetitive code, such as implementations of interfaces for different types, serialization/deserialization logic, or data structure accessors.

Data-Driven Code Generation: Generate code based on external data sources (e.g., configuration files, data schemas) processed at compile time.

Compile-Time Reflection (Limited): Use @Type and introspection capabilities to generate code that adapts to the structure of different types.

Example: Generating Equality Functions for Structs:

Code snippet

```
const std = @import("std");

comptime fn generateEqualityFn(comptime T: type) []const u8 {
    if (@typeInfo(T) != .Struct) {
        return ""; // Only generate for structs
    }

    var builder = std.build.Builder.init(std.heap.page_allocator);
    defer builder.deinit();

    try builder.append("{} == {}", .{@typeName(T), @typeName(T)});
```

```zig
    try builder.append("(a: *const {}, b: *const {}) bool {\n",
.{@typeName(T), @typeName(T)});
    try builder.append("    return \n");

    var first = true;
    inline for (@typeInfo(T).Struct.fields) |field| {
        if (!first) {
            try builder.append(" and\n");
        }
            try builder.append("        a.{} == b.{}", .{field.name,
field.name});
        first = false;
    }

    try builder.append(";\n}\n");
    return builder.finish();
}

// Define some structs
pub const Point = struct { x: i32, y: i32 };
pub const Color = struct { r: u8, g: u8, b: u8 };

// Generate equality functions at compile time
comptime {
    const point_eq_src = generateEqualityFn(Point);
    if (point_eq_src.len > 0) {
        @eval(@compileLog(point_eq_src));
    }

    const color_eq_src = generateEqualityFn(Color);
    if (color_eq_src.len > 0) {
        @eval(@compileLog(color_eq_src));
    }
}
```

```
pub fn main() !void {
    const p1 = Point{ .x = 1, .y = 2 };
    const p2 = Point{ .x = 1, .y = 2 };
    const p3 = Point{ .x = 3, .y = 4 };
    std.debug.print("p1 == p2: {}\n", .{p1 == p2}); // true
    std.debug.print("p1 == p3: {}\n", .{p1 == p3}); // false

    const c1 = Color{ .r = 255, .g = 0, .b = 0 };
    const c2 = Color{ .r = 255, .g = 0, .b = 0 };
    std.debug.print("c1 == c2: {}\n", .{c1 == c2}); // true
}
```

Limitations and Considerations:

Compile-Time Execution Only: Metaprogramming in Zig happens entirely at compile time. You cannot generate or modify code at runtime.

Complexity: Metaprogramming can sometimes make code harder to read and understand if not used judiciously.

Build Time: Excessive compile-time computations can increase build times.

Limited Reflection: Zig's reflection capabilities are primarily focused on types and their layout. More advanced runtime reflection is not a core feature.

Benefits of Metaprogramming in Zig:

Performance: Generate specialized code that avoids runtime overhead.

Code Reduction: Automate the generation of repetitive boilerplate.

Type Safety: Perform checks and generate code based on type information at compile time, improving safety.

Flexibility: Adapt code based on compile-time configurations and data.

Metaprogramming in Zig is a powerful tool that allows you to write more expressive and efficient code. By leveraging `comptime` functions, type introspection, and code generation techniques, you can automate many aspects of software development and create highly optimized and adaptable applications. However, it's important to use these features thoughtfully to maintain code clarity and manage build times.

10.2 Cross-Compilation and Deployment Strategies for Different Platforms

Let's explore **Cross-Compilation and Deployment Strategies for Different Platforms** using Zig. Zig is exceptionally well-suited for cross-compilation due to its design and build system.[1]

1. Cross-Compilation with Zig:

Cross-compilation is the process of compiling code on one platform (the build host) to create an executable that can run on a different platform (the target).[2] Zig makes this remarkably straightforward.

Target Triples: Zig uses target triples to identify specific platforms.[3] A target triple typically consists of the architecture, the operating system, and the ABI (Application Binary Interface). Examples:

`x86_64-linux-gnu`: 64-bit x86 architecture, Linux operating system, GNU ABI (common on many Linux distributions).

`aarch64-linux-gnu`: 64-bit ARM architecture, Linux operating system, GNU ABI (common on ARM Linux devices).[4]

`x86_64-windows-msvc`: 64-bit x86 architecture, Windows operating system, Microsoft Visual C++ ABI.

`aarch64-darwin`: 64-bit ARM architecture, macOS operating system.

`wasm32-freestanding-musl`: 32-bit WebAssembly, no specific OS, MUSL libc.

`-target` **Flag:** You specify the target platform during compilation using the `-target` flag with the `zig build` or `zig build-exe` commands.

Bash

```
# Build for 64-bit Linux
zig build-exe your_program.zig -target x86_64-linux-gnu -O ReleaseFast

# Build for 64-bit Windows
zig build-exe your_program.zig -target x86_64-windows-msvc -O ReleaseFast

# Build for 64-bit macOS (ARM)
zig build-exe your_program.zig -target aarch64-darwin -O ReleaseFast
```

```
# Build for WebAssembly
zig build-exe your_program.zig -target wasm32-freestanding-musl
-O ReleaseFast
```

Standard Library Support: Zig's standard library is designed to be cross-platform.[5] When you target a different platform, Zig will compile the appropriate parts of the standard library for that target.

No External Dependencies (Often): Zig strives to minimize external dependencies.[6] This greatly simplifies cross-compilation as you often don't need to install cross-compilers or SDKs for other platforms separately (Zig includes them).

2. Deployment Strategies for Different Platforms:

Once you have your cross-compiled executables, you need strategies to deploy them to the target platforms. The best strategy depends heavily on the target OS and the nature of your application.

2.1. Desktop Applications (Linux, Windows, macOS):

Self-Contained Executables: Zig often produces self-contained executables that bundle necessary runtime components (though you might still need system libraries depending on your dependencies).[7] This simplifies deployment as users typically just need to download and run the executable.

Package Managers (Linux): For Linux, consider packaging your application in formats like .deb (Debian/Ubuntu), .rpm (Red

Hat/Fedora/CentOS), or `.apk` (Alpine). This allows users to install and manage your application through their system's package manager. Tools like `fpm` can help with creating these packages.

Installers (Windows, macOS): For Windows, creating an installer (e.g., using tools like Inno Setup or NSIS) provides a guided installation experience for users. For macOS, you can create `.app` bundles or `.pkg` installers using Xcode or third-party tools.[8]

Distribution Platforms: Consider distributing your application through platform-specific app stores (e.g., the Microsoft Store, the macOS App Store, or Linux app stores like Flathub and Snapcraft). This can provide wider reach and easier updates for users.

Web Delivery: For some desktop applications, especially those with update mechanisms, you might distribute the executable directly from your website.

2.2. WebAssembly (Wasm):

Integration with Web Pages: Wasm modules are typically loaded and executed within a web browser using JavaScript.[9] You'll need to write JavaScript code to interact with your Wasm module (e.g., passing data, calling functions, rendering output to the DOM).[10]

Wasm Runtimes (Outside Browsers): Wasm can also run in standalone environments using Wasm runtimes like Node.js (with wasmedge), Wasmer, or Wasmtime.[11] Deployment here involves providing the `.wasm` file and potentially any necessary host bindings or configurations.

Server-Side Wasm: Wasm can be used on the server-side for various purposes, such as running plugins or computationally intensive tasks in a sandboxed environment.[12] Deployment would depend on the specific server-side Wasm runtime being used.

2.3. Embedded Systems and Bare Metal:

Firmware Images: For embedded systems, you'll often compile your Zig code into a firmware image (e.g., `.bin`, `.hex`) that can be flashed onto the device's microcontroller or processor.

Bootloaders: You might need to work with bootloaders to load and execute your firmware.

Hardware-Specific SDKs: Interacting with hardware often requires using platform-specific SDKs or libraries.[13] You might need to conditionally compile code based on the target architecture and operating system (or lack thereof). Zig's `builtin` module and conditional compilation (`if`) can be helpful here.

Deployment Tools: Deployment often involves using specialized tools provided by the hardware vendor for flashing or transferring the firmware to the device.

2.4. Mobile (Android, iOS - More Complex with Zig Currently):

Native Development: While Zig can theoretically target these platforms (e.g., through the Android NDK or by targeting Darwin for iOS), the ecosystem and tooling for building full-fledged mobile apps with Zig are less mature compared to languages like Kotlin/Java (Android) and Swift/Objective-C (iOS).

Cross-Platform Frameworks: You might consider using cross-platform frameworks that have Zig bindings or support Wasm, which could then run on mobile. However, this adds another layer of complexity.

Focus on Libraries: Zig might be more immediately useful for building high-performance libraries that can be integrated into mobile apps written in the platform's native languages.

3. General Deployment Considerations:

Dependencies: Be aware of any runtime dependencies your Zig application might have (e.g., system libraries). While Zig aims for self-contained binaries, you might link against external C libraries that need to be present on the target system.

File Size: Optimize your builds for size if deployment bandwidth or storage on the target device is a concern (use `-O ReleaseSmall` or `-O ReleaseFast` for release builds).

Security: Consider security implications during deployment, especially for networked applications or those handling sensitive data.

Updates: Plan for how you will deliver updates to your application on different platforms. Package managers and app stores often handle updates automatically.[14] For self-distributed applications, you might need to implement your own update mechanism.

Testing on Target Platforms: Thoroughly test your cross-compiled executables on the actual target platforms to ensure they function correctly. Emulators and simulators can be helpful but might not always perfectly replicate real-world conditions.

In summary, Zig provides excellent cross-compilation capabilities through its `-target` flag and included toolchains.[15] Deployment strategies vary significantly depending on the target platform, ranging from self-contained executables for desktops to firmware images for embedded systems and integration with web pages for

WebAssembly. Understanding the nuances of each platform is key to a successful deployment. As the Zig ecosystem evolves, we might see more streamlined tools and practices for mobile and other platforms.

10.3 Best Practices for Structuring Large Zig Projects and Contributing to the Ecosystem

Alright, let's discuss **Best Practices for Structuring Large Zig Projects and Contributing to the Ecosystem**. As your Zig projects grow in size and complexity, a well-defined structure becomes crucial for maintainability, collaboration, and scalability. Similarly, contributing to the Zig ecosystem can help the language and community thrive.

Part 1: Structuring Large Zig Projects

1.**Clear Entry Point (**`src/main.zig`**):**

The `src/main.zig` file should serve as the primary entry point for your executable. It should contain the `main` function.

Keep this file relatively clean, primarily responsible for setting up and calling into other modules.

2. **Modular Design (**`src/`**):**

Organize your code into logical modules within the `src/` directory. Each module should encapsulate a specific area of functionality.

Use subdirectories within `src/` to further group related modules.

Example:

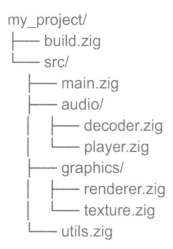

```
my_project/
├── build.zig
└── src/
    ├── main.zig
    ├── audio/
    │   ├── decoder.zig
    │   └── player.zig
    ├── graphics/
    │   ├── renderer.zig
    │   └── texture.zig
    └── utils.zig
```

1.Explicit Imports:

Always explicitly import the modules you need using `@import`. This makes dependencies clear and avoids namespace pollution.

Use short, descriptive aliases for imported modules if needed for brevity.

2.Code snippet

const audio = @import("./audio/player.zig");

```
const renderer = @import("./graphics/renderer.zig");
const utils = @import("utils.zig");
3.
```

4. **Public vs. Private API:**

Use pub to mark symbols (functions, structs, variables, etc.) that are intended to be part of the module's public API.

Keep internal implementation details private (without pub) to prevent accidental external dependencies and allow for easier refactoring.

5. **Testing Alongside Code (**`src/your_module_test.zig`**):**

Place unit tests for a module in a separate file named `your_module_test.zig` within the same directory as `your_module.zig`. This makes it easy to find and run tests.

Use @import to access the module being tested.

6. Code snippet

```
// src/audio/player.zig
pub fn playSound(file: []const u8) void {
    // ... implementation ...
```

```
}

// src/audio/player_test.zig
const std = @import("std");
const assert = std.debug.assert;
const player = @import("./player.zig");

test "audio player can play a sound" {
    player.playSound("test.wav");
    // ... assertions about the side effects or behavior ...
}
7.
```

8. **Build Configuration** (`build.zig`):

The `build.zig` file is crucial for defining how your project is built, including:

Adding executable targets.

Adding library targets (for reusable code).

Specifying dependencies (internal and external).

Defining build steps (e.g., running tests, generating documentation).

Allowing configuration options for users.

Keep your `build.zig` organized and well-documented.

9. **Dependency Management (External Libraries):**

For external dependencies, use a package manager like ZPM (Zig Package Manager) or integrate with Git submodules.

Update and manage dependencies carefully.

Document your dependencies in a `README` or a dedicated dependency file.

10. **Documentation:**

Use Zig's documentation comment syntax (`///`) to document public APIs (structs, functions, etc.). This allows tools to generate documentation for your project.

Provide a comprehensive `README.md` at the root of your project explaining its purpose, how to build and run it, and any important concepts.

11. **Code Formatting and Style:**

Adhere to a consistent code style. Consider using a code formatter if one becomes widely adopted in the Zig community. Consistency improves readability.

12. **Example Code (**`examples/`**):**

Include an `examples/` directory with small, focused examples demonstrating how to use different parts of your library or application.

Part 2: Contributing to the Zig Ecosystem

1.Engage with the Community:

Join the official Zig Discord server, the Zig Discourse forum, and other community channels.

Ask questions, share your knowledge, and participate in discussions.

2. **Report Issues:**

If you find bugs in the Zig compiler, standard library, or other Zig projects, report them clearly and concisely on the respective issue trackers (usually GitHub). Provide steps to reproduce the issue.

3. **Submit Patches (Pull Requests):**

If you have a fix for a bug or a new feature you'd like to contribute, submit a pull request (PR) on GitHub.

Follow the contribution guidelines of the project you're contributing to.

Keep your PRs focused and well-described.

Be prepared to receive feedback and iterate on your contribution.

4. **Contribute to the Standard Library:**

The Zig standard library is a crucial part of the ecosystem. Consider contributing new modules, improving existing ones, or fixing bugs. This often involves more in-depth discussion and adherence to the library's design principles.

5. **Develop and Share Libraries:**

If you build a useful library, consider open-sourcing it and sharing it with the community (e.g., through ZPM or by announcing it on community channels).

Provide good documentation and examples for your libraries.

6. **Write Tutorials and Articles:**

Help others learn Zig by writing tutorials, blog posts, or articles about specific topics or projects.

7. Help Maintain Projects:

If you become familiar with a Zig project, offer to help maintain it by reviewing PRs, triaging issues, and contributing to its development.

8. Follow the Zig Code of Conduct:

Be respectful and considerate in all your interactions with the Zig community.

9. Use Zig and Provide Feedback:

The best way to contribute is often by using Zig in your own projects and providing feedback on your experience, including what works well and what could be improved.

10. Be Patient and Persistent:

Contributing to open-source projects takes time and effort. Be patient, persistent, and willing to learn.

By following these best practices for structuring your own Zig projects, you'll create more maintainable and collaborative codebases. By actively participating in the Zig ecosystem, you'll help the language grow and benefit the entire community.

Remember that the Zig community is generally welcoming and eager to help newcomers and contributors.

www.ingramcontent.com/pod-product-compliance
Lightning Source LLC
LaVergne TN
LVHW012334060326
832902LV00012B/1886